A POCKET GUIDE

A Young Earth

Evidence that supports the biblical perspective

ROBLEMS WITH RADIOACTIVE DATING • CARBON-14 DATING • WHERE DID THE IDEA OF "MILLIONS OF YEARS" COME FROM? • HOW OLD IS THE EARTH? • THE HEAVENS DECLARE A YOUNG SOLAR SYSTEM

A POCKET GUIDE TO . . .

A Young Earth

Evidence that supports the biblical perspective

1:1

answersingenesis

Petersburg, Kentucky, USA

Third printing February 2012

ISBN: 1-60092-303-8

Printed in China

www.answersingenesis.org

Table of Contents

Introduction

The question of the age of the earth has produced heated discussions on debate boards, in classrooms, on TV and radio, and in many churches, Christian colleges, and seminaries. The primary sides are young-earth proponents (biblical age of the earth and universe of about 6,000 years) and old-earth proponents (secular age of the earth and universe of about 4.5 billion years and 14 billion years, respectively).

The difference could not be greater! Where do these ideas come from, and upon what authority are they based? Can we accurately calculate an age for the earth?

From the earliest times, man has tried to estimate the age of the earth from historical records, secular chronologies, biblical sources, and more recently from scientific measurements. Only in the past few decades have secular scientists come to agreement based on radiometric dating methods. But are these methods accurate? Are there other methods for measuring the age of the earth that give different results?

This *Pocket Guide to a Young Earth* will aid you in understanding the debate, the dating methods, the problems with these methods, and upon what authority the different views are based. You will find that when we start from biblical assumptions, and look at the world through the lens of Scripture, we can come to solid conclusions that are not only true to the scriptural record, but also agree with sound science.

Radiometric Dating, Part 1

Back to Basics

by Andrew A. Snelling

Most people think that radioactive dating has proven the earth is billions of years old. After all, textbooks, media, and museums glibly present ages of millions of years as fact.

Yet few people know how radiometric dating works or bother to ask what assumptions drive the conclusions. So let's take a closer look and see how reliable this dating method really is.

Atoms—basics we observe today

Each chemical element, such as carbon and oxygen, consists of atoms. Each atom is thought to be made up of three basic parts.

The nucleus contains protons (tiny particles each with a single positive electric charge) and neutrons (particles without any electric charge). Orbiting around the nucleus are electrons (tiny particles each with a single negative electric charge).

The atoms of each element may vary slightly in the numbers of neutrons within their nuclei. These variations are called isotopes of that element. While the number of neutrons varies, every atom of any element always has the same number of protons and electrons.

So, for example, every carbon atom contains six protons and six electrons, but the number of neutrons in each nucleus can be six, seven, or even eight. Therefore, carbon has three isotopes (variations), which are specified carbon-12, carbon-13, and carbon-14 (Figure 1).

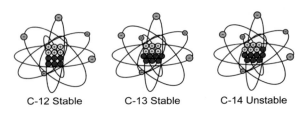

C-12 Stable	C-13 Stable	C-14 Unstable

Figure 1: Stable & unstable atoms: Radiometric dating is based on a simple fact about atoms. If an atom has too many neutrons in its nucleus (blue circle below), it is unstable and will change into a stable form. To date a sample, scientists calculate how much time would be required for the unstable atoms in the sample to change into a stable form.

For example, most carbon atoms are stable because they have only six or seven neutrons in their nuclei (carbon-12 and carbon-13, above). But some carbon atoms have too many neutrons and are unstable (carbon-14).

⊕ Proton
⬤ Neutron
⊖ Electron

Radioactive decay

Some isotopes are radioactive; that is, they are unstable because their nuclei are too large. To achieve stability, the atom must make adjustments, particularly in its nucleus. In some cases, the isotopes eject particles, primarily neutrons and protons. (These are the moving particles measured by Geiger counters and the like.) The end result is a stable atom, but of a *different* chemical element (not carbon) because the atom now has a *different* number of protons and electrons.

This process of changing one element (designated as the parent isotope) into another element (referred to as the daughter isotope) is called radioactive decay. The parent isotopes that decay are called radioisotopes.

Actually, it isn't really a decay process in the normal sense of the word, like the decay of fruit. The daughter atoms are not lesser in quality than the parent atoms from which they were produced. Both are complete atoms in every sense of the word.

Geologists regularly use five parent isotopes to date rocks: uranium-238, uranium-235, potassium-40, rubidium-87, and samarium-147. These parent radioisotopes change into daughter lead-206, lead-207, argon-40, strontium-87, and neodymium-143 isotopes, respectively. Thus geologists refer to uranium-lead (two versions), potassium-argon, rubidium-strontium, or samarium-neodymium dates for rocks. Note that the carbon-14 (or radio-carbon) method is not used to date rocks because most rocks do not contain carbon.

Chemical analysis of rocks today

Geologists can't use just any old rock for dating. They must find rocks that have the isotopes listed above, even if these isotopes are present only in minute amounts. Most often, this is a rock body, or unit, that has formed from the cooling of molten rock material (called magma). Examples are granites (formed by cooling under the ground) and basalts (formed by cooling of lava at the earth's surface).

The next step is to measure the amount of the parent and daughter isotopes in a sample of the rock unit. Specially equipped laboratories can do this with accuracy and precision. So, in general, few people quarrel with the resulting chemical analyses.

It is the interpretation of these chemical analyses that raises potential problems. To understand how geologists "read" the age of a rock from these chemical analyses, let's use the analogy of an hourglass "clock" (Figure 2).

In an hourglass, grains of fine sand fall at a steady rate from the top bowl to the bottom. After one hour, all the sand has fallen into the bottom bowl. So, after only half an hour, half the sand should be in the top bowl, and the other half should be in the bottom bowl.

Suppose that a person did not observe when the hourglass was turned over. He walks into the room when half the sand is in the

Figure 2: Wrong assumptions, wrong dates

Unstable atoms, such as uranium (U), eventually change into stable atoms, such as lead (Pb). The original version is called a parent atom (or isotope), and the new version is called a daughter atom.

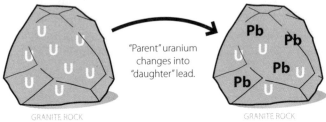

"Parent" uranium changes into "daughter" lead.

GRANITE ROCK

GRANITE ROCK

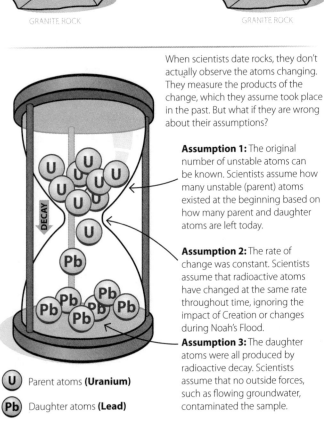

DECAY

U Parent atoms (**Uranium**)

Pb Daughter atoms (**Lead**)

When scientists date rocks, they don't actually observe the atoms changing. They measure the products of the change, which they assume took place in the past. But what if they are wrong about their assumptions?

Assumption 1: The original number of unstable atoms can be known. Scientists assume how many unstable (parent) atoms existed at the beginning based on how many parent and daughter atoms are left today.

Assumption 2: The rate of change was constant. Scientists assume that radioactive atoms have changed at the same rate throughout time, ignoring the impact of Creation or changes during Noah's Flood.

Assumption 3: The daughter atoms were all produced by radioactive decay. Scientists assume that no outside forces, such as flowing groundwater, contaminated the sample.

top bowl, and half the sand is in the bottom bowl. Most people would assume that the "clock" started half an hour earlier.

By way of analogy, the sand grains in the top bowl represent atoms of the parent radioisotope (uranium-238, potassium-40, etc.) (*Figure 2*). The falling sand represents radioactive decay, and the sand at the bottom represents the daughter isotope (lead-206, argon-40, etc).

When a geologist tests a rock sample, he assumes all the daughter atoms were produced by the decay of the parent since the rock formed. So if he knows the rate at which the parent decays, he can calculate how long it took for the daughter (measured in the rock today) to form.

But what if the assumptions are wrong? For example, what if radioactive material was added to the top bowl or if the decay rate has changed? Future articles will explore the assumptions that can lead to incorrect dates and how the Bible's history helps us make better sense of the patterns of radioactive "dates" we find in the rocks today.

Dr. Andrew Snelling is one of the world's most respected creation scientists specializing in geology. He is the director of the Research Division at Answers in Genesis–USA and editor-in-chief of *Answers Research Journal*.

Dr. Snelling completed a BS degree in Applied Geology at the University of New South Wales (Sydney, Australia). He earned a PhD in geology from the University of Sydney. Dr. Snelling has worked as a consultant research geologist to organizations in both Australia and the U.S, and is the author of numerous scientific articles.

Dr. Snelling is a member of many professional organizations, including the Geological Society of Australia, the Geological Society of America, and the Creation Research Society.

Radiometric Dating, Part 2

Problems with the Assumptions

by Andrew A. Snelling

Most people think that radioactive dating has proven the earth is billions of years old. Yet this view is based on a misunderstanding of how radiometric dating works. The previous chapter explained how scientists observe unstable atoms changing into stable atoms in the present. This chapter explains how scientists run into problems when they make assumptions about what happened in the unobserved past.

The hourglass "clock"—an analogy for dating rocks

An hourglass is a helpful analogy to explain how geologists calculate the ages of rocks. When we look at sand in an hourglass, we can estimate how much time has passed based on the amount of sand that has fallen to the bottom.

Radioactive rocks offer a similar "clock." Radioactive atoms, such as uranium (the parent isotopes), decay into stable atoms, such as lead (the daughter isotopes), at a measurable rate. To date a radioactive rock, geologists first measure the "sand grains" in the top glass bowl (the parent radioisotope, such as uranium-238 or potassium-40).

They also measure the sand grains in the bottom bowl (the daughter isotope, such as lead-206 or argon-40, respectively). Based on these observations and the known rate of radioactive decay, they estimate the time it has taken for the daughter isotope to accumulate in the rock.

However, unlike the hourglass whose accuracy can be tested by turning it upside down and comparing it to trustworthy clocks, the reliability of the radioactive "clock" is subject to three unprovable assumptions. No geologist was present when the rocks were formed to see their contents, and no geologist was present to measure how fast the radioactive "clock" has been running through the millions of years that supposedly passed after the rock was formed.

Assumption 1: conditions at time zero

No geologists were present when most rocks formed, so they cannot test whether the original rocks already contained daughter isotopes alongside their parent radioisotopes. For example, with regard to the volcanic lavas that erupted, flowed, and cooled to form rocks in the unobserved past, evolutionary geologists simply assume that none of the daughter argon-40 atoms were in the lava rocks.

For the other radioactive "clocks," it is assumed that by analyzing multiple samples of a rock body, or unit, today it is possible to determine how much of the daughter isotopes (lead, strontium, or neodymium) were present when the rock formed (via the so-called isochron technique, which is still based on unproven assumptions 2 and 3).

Yet lava flows that have occurred in the present have been tested soon after they erupted, and they invariably contained much more argon-40 than expected.[1] For example, when a sample of the lava in the Mt. St. Helens crater (that had been observed to form and cool in 1986) (Figure 1) was analyzed in 1996, it contained so much argon-40 that it had a calculated "age" of 350,000 years![2] Similarly, lava flows on the sides of Mt. Ngauruhoe, New Zealand (Figure 2), known to be less than 50 years old, yielded "ages" of up to 3.5 million years.[3]

So it is logical to conclude that if recent lava flows of *known* age yield incorrect old potassium-argon ages due to the extra argon-40 that they inherited from the erupting volcanoes, then ancient lava flows of unknown ages could likewise have inherited extra argon-40 and yield excessively old ages.

There are similar problems with the other radioactive "clocks." For example, consider the dating of Grand Canyon's basalts (rocks formed by lava cooling at the earth's surface). We find places on the North Rim where volcanoes erupted after the

Assumption—conditions at time zero

Scientists do not know how many "daughter atoms" were present when most rocks first formed. So when they test rocks produced by lava flows in recent years, their bad assumptions yield old "ages."

FIGURE 1

Bad results: "old" dates for recent eruptions

A rock formed at Mount St. Helens in 1986 yielded a radiometric age of 350,000 years.

FIGURE 2

A rock formed by lava flows at Mt. Ngauruhoe in 1954 yielded a radiometric age of 3.5 million years.

FIGURE 3

A rock at the top of Grand Canyon, formed by a recent volcanic eruption, yielded the same age as volcanic rocks deep below the canyon wall—1.143 billion years.

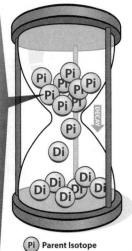

(Pi) **Parent Isotope**

(Di) **Daughter Isotope**

FIGURE 1: USGS/Cascades Volcano Observatory   FIGURES 2–5: courtesy Andrew Snelling

Canyon was formed, sending lavas cascading over the walls and down into the Canyon.

Obviously, these eruptions took place very recently, after the Canyon's layers were deposited (Figure 3). These basalts yield ages of up to 1 million years based on the amounts of potassium and argon isotopes in the rocks. But when we date the rocks using the rubidium and strontium isotopes, we get an age of 1.143 billion years. This is the same age that we get for the basalt layers deep below the walls of the eastern Grand Canyon.[4]

How could both lavas—one at the top and one at the bottom of the Canyon—be the same age based on these parent and daughter isotopes? One solution is that both the recent and early lava flows inherited the same rubidium-strontium chemistry—not age—from the same source, deep in the earth's upper mantle. This source already had both rubidium and strontium.

To make matters even worse for the claimed reliability of these radiometric dating methods, these same basalts that flowed from the top of the Canyon yield a samarium-neodymium age of about 916 million years,[5] and a uranium-lead age of about 2.6 billion years![6]

Assumption 2: no contamination

The problems with contamination, as with inheritance, are already well-documented in the textbooks on radioactive dating of rocks.[7] Unlike the hourglass, where its two bowls are sealed, the radioactive "clock" in rocks is open to contamination by gain or loss of parent or daughter isotopes because of waters flowing in the ground from rainfall and from the molten rocks beneath volcanoes. Similarly, as molten lava rises through a conduit from deep inside the earth to be erupted through a volcano, pieces of the conduit wallrocks and their isotopes can mix into the lava and contaminate it.

Because of such contamination, the less than 50-year-old lava flows at Mt. Ngauruhoe, New Zealand (Figure 4), yield a rubidium-strontium "age" of 133 million years, a samarium-neodymium "age" of 197 million years, and a uranium-lead "age" of 3.908 billion years![8]

Assumption 3: constant decay rate

Physicists have carefully measured the radioactive decay rates of parent radioisotopes in laboratories over the last 100 or so years and have found them to be essentially constant (within the

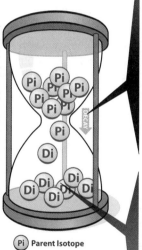

(Pi) Parent Isotope

(Di) Daughter Isotope

Assumption—constant decay rate

Scientists do not know how quickly radioactive atoms decayed in the past. So they assume a constant rate. But when they tested zircon crystals from a borehole in New Mexico, they found two very different dates, depending on what measurement they used.

Bad results: contradictory decay rates

Measuring the uranium in these crystals yields an "age" of 1.5 billion years. But measuring the amount of helium that leaked out as a result of the decay yields an age of 6,000 years.

FIGURE 5

Assumption—no contamination

Scientist do not know how much the rocks have been contaminated. So they usually assume no contamination.

Bad results: different dates from the same rocks

FIGURE 4

Contamination of lava flows at Mt. Ngauruhoe, known to be less than 50 years old, yielded three different "ages" for rocks—133 million years, 197 million years, and 3.908 billion years.

measurement error margins). Furthermore, they have not been able to significantly change these decay rates by heat, pressure, or electrical and magnetic fields. So geologists have assumed these radioactive decay rates have been constant for billions of years.

However, this is an enormous extrapolation of seven orders of magnitude back through immense spans of unobserved time without any concrete proof that such an extrapolation is credible. Nevertheless, geologists insist the radioactive decay rates have always been constant, because it makes these radioactive clocks "work"!

New evidence, however, has recently been discovered that can only be explained by the radioactive decay rates *not* having been constant in the past.[9] For example, the radioactive decay of uranium in tiny crystals in a New Mexico granite (Figure 5) yields a uranium-lead "age" of 1.5 billion years. Yet the *same* uranium decay also produced abundant helium, but only 6,000 years worth of that helium was found to have leaked out of the tiny crystals.

This means that the uranium must have decayed very rapidly over the same 6,000 years that the helium was leaking. The rate of uranium decay must have been at least 250,000 times faster than today's measured rate![10]

The assumptions on which the radioactive dating is based are not only unprovable but plagued with problems. As this article has illustrated, rocks may have inherited parent and daughter isotopes from their sources, or they may have been contaminated when they moved through other rocks to their current locations. Or inflowing water may have mixed isotopes into the rocks. In addition, the radioactive decay rates have not been constant.

So if these clocks are based on faulty assumptions and yield unreliable results, then scientists should not trust or promote the claimed radioactive "ages" of countless millions of years, especially since they contradict the true history of the universe as recorded in God's Word.

1. A. A. Snelling, "Geochemical Processes in the Mantle and Crust," in *Radioisotopes and the Age of the Earth: A Young-Earth Creationist Research Initiative*, L. Vardiman, A. A. Snelling, and E. F. Chaffin, eds. (El Cajon, California: Institute for Creation Research; St. Joseph, Missouri: Creation Research Society, 2000), pp. 123–304.

2. S. A. Austin, "Excess Argon within Mineral Concentrates from the New Dacite Lava Dome at Mount St. Helens Volcano," *Creation Ex Nihilo Technical Journal* 10.3 (1996): 335–343.

3. A. A. Snelling, "The Cause of Anomalous Potassium-Argon 'Ages' for Recent Andesite Flows at Mt. Ngauruhoe, New Zealand, and the Implications for Potassium-Argon 'Dating,'" in *Proceedings of the Fourth International Conference on Creationism*, ed. R. E. Walsh (Pittsburgh: Creation Science Fellowship, 1998), pp. 503–525.

4. A. A. Snelling, "Isochron Discordances and the Role of Inheritance and Mixing of Radioisotopes in the Mantle and Crust," in *Radioisotopes and the Age of the Earth: Results of a Young-Earth Creationist Research Initiative*, eds. L. Vardiman, A. A. Snelling, and E. F. Chaffin (El Cajon, California: Institute for Creation Research; Chino Valley, Arizona: Creation Research Society, 2005), pp. 393–524; D. B. DeYoung, "Radioisotope Dating Case Studies" in *Thousands . . . Not Billions* (Green Forest, Arkansas: Master Books, 2005), pp. 123–139.

5. Ref. 4, 2005.

6. S. A. Austin, ed., *Grand Canyon: Monument to Catastrophe* (Santee, California: Institute for Creation Research, 1994), pp. 123–126.

7. G. Faure and T. M. Mensing, *Isotopes: Principles and Applications*, 3rd ed. (Hoboken, New Jersey: John Wiley & Sons, Hoboken, 2005); A. P. Dickin, *Radiogenic Isotope Geology*, 2nd ed. (UK: Cambridge University Press, 2005).

8. A. A. Snelling, "The Relevance of Rb-Sr, Sm-Nd and Pb-Pb Isotope Systematics to Elucidation of the Genesis and History of Recent Andesite Flows at Mt. Ngauruhoe, New Zealand, and the Implications for Radioisotopic Dating," in *Proceedings of the Fifth International Conference on Creationism*, ed. R. L. Ivey, Jr. (Pittsburgh: Creation Science Fellowship, 2003), pp. 285–303; Ref. 4, 2005.

9. L. Vardiman, A. A. Snelling, and E. F. Chaffin, eds., *Radioisotopes and the Age of the Earth: Results of a Young-Earth Creationist Research Initiative* (El Cajon, California: Institute for Creation Research; Chino Valley, Arizona: Creation Research Society, 2005); D. B. DeYoung, *Thousands . . . Not Billions* (Green Forest, Arkansas: Master Books, 2005).

10. For more details, see Don DeYoung, *Thousands . . . Not Billions* (Green Forest, Arkansas: Master Books, 2005), pp. 65–78.

Radiometric Dating, Part 3
Making Sense of the Patterns

by Andrew A. Snelling

*T*he last chapter showed that the same rocks can yield very different ages, depending on which radiometric dating technique you use. These inconsistent results are due to the problems of inheritance and contamination, which cause the rocks' chemistry to differ from the assumptions of standard radioactive "clocks."

Furthermore, new evidence indicates that radioactive elements in the rocks, which are used to date the rocks, decayed at much faster rates during some past event (or events) in the last 6,000 years. So the claimed ages of many millions of years, which are based on today's slow decay rates, are totally unreliable.

Does this mean we should throw out the radioactive clocks? Surprisingly, they are useful!

The general principles of using radioisotopes to date rocks are sound; it's just that the assumptions have been wrong and led to exaggerated dates. While the clocks cannot yield absolute dates for rocks, they can provide relative ages that allow us to compare any two rock units and know which one formed first.

They also allow us to compare rock units in different areas of the world to find which ones formed at the same time. Furthermore, if physicists examine why the same rocks yield different dates, they may discover new clues about the unusual behavior of radioactive elements during the past.

With the help of this growing body of information, creation geologists hope to piece together a better understanding of the precise sequence of events in earth's history, from Creation Week to the Flood and beyond.

Different dates for the same rocks

Usually geologists do not use all four main radioactive clocks to date a rock unit. This is considered an unnecessary waste of time and money. After all, if these clocks really do work, then they should all yield the same age for a given rock unit. Sometimes though, using different parent radioisotopes to date different samples (or minerals) from the same rock unit does yield different ages, hinting that something is amiss.[1]

Recently, creationist researchers have utilized all four common radioactive clocks to date the same samples from the same rock units.[2] Among these were four rock units far down in the Grand Canyon rock sequence (Figure 1), chosen because they are well known and characterized. These were as follows: •

Radiometric Ages of rock samples. Samples from the same rock unit can yield very different radiometric "ages," depending on the atoms being measured. The table below shows varying "ages" from rock units found in the Grand Canyon. Why is there so much variation? The measurements are not wrong, so there is only one reasonable answer: each radioactive element decayed at a different, faster rate in the past!

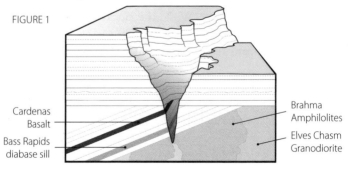

FIGURE 1

Cardenas Basalt

Bass Rapids diabase sill

Brahma Amphilolites

Elves Chasm Granodiorite

- Cardenas Basalt (lava flows deep in the east Canyon sequence) (Figure 2).

- Bass Rapids diabase sill (where basalt magma squeezed between layers and cooled) (Figure 3).

- Brahma amphibolites (basalt lava flows deep in the Canyon sequence that later metamorphosed) (Figure 4).

FIGURE 2—Cardenas Basalt

FIGURE 3—Bass Rapids diabase sill

FIGURE 4—Brahma amphibolites

FIGURE 5—Elves Chasm Granodiorite

Rock Unit	Ages (million years)			
	Potassium-argon	Rubidium-strontium	Uranium-lead	Samarium-neodymium
Cardenas Basalt	516 (±30)	1111 (±81)	—	1588 (±170)
Bass Rapids diabase sill	842 (±164)	1060 (±24)	1250 (±130)	1379 (±140)
Brahma Amphibolites	—	1240 (±84)	1883 (±53)	1655 (±40)
Elves Chasm Granodiorite	—	1512 (±140)	1933 (±220)	1664 (±200)

TABLE 1—Radioactive ages yielded by four Grand Canyon rock units. (The error margins are shown in parentheses.)

- Elves Chasm Granodiorite (a granite regarded as the oldest Canyon rock unit) (Figure 5).

Table 1 lists the dates obtained from each rock unit.

It is immediately apparent that the ages for each rock unit do not agree. Indeed, in the Cardenas Basalt, for example, the samarium-neodymium age is *three times* the potassium-argon age.

Nevertheless, the ages follow three obvious patterns. Two techniques (potassium-argon age and rubidium-strontium) *always* yield younger ages than two other techniques (uranium-lead and samarium-neodymium). Furthermore, the potassium-argon ages are *always* younger than the rubidium-strontium ages. And often the samarium-neodymium ages are younger than the uranium-lead ages.

What then do these patterns mean? All the radioactive clocks in each rock unit should have started "ticking" at the same time, the instant that each rock unit was formed. So how do we explain that they have each recorded different ages?

The answer is simple but profound. Each of the radioactive elements must have decayed at different, faster rates in the past!

In the case of the Cardenas Basalt, while the potassium-argon clock ticked through 516 million years, two other clocks ticked through 1,111 million years and 1,588 million years. So if these clocks ticked at such different rates in the past, not only are they inaccurate, but these rocks may not be millions of years old!

But how could radioactive decay rates have been different in the past? Creationist researchers don't fully understand yet. However, the observed age patterns provide clues. Potassium and rubidium decay radioactively by the process known as beta (β) decay, whereas uranium and neodymium decay via alpha (α) decay. The former *always* gives younger ages. We see another pattern *within* beta decay. Potassium today decays faster than rubidium and *always* gives younger ages.

Both of these patterns suggest something happened in the past inside the nuclei of these parent atoms to accelerate their decay. The decay rate varied based on the stability or instability of the parent atoms. Research is continuing.

Relative ages

Look again at Figure 1, which is a geologic diagram depicting the rock layers in the walls of the Grand Canyon, along with the rock units deep in the inner gorge along the Colorado River. This diagram shows that the radiometric dating methods accurately show the top rock layer is younger than the layers beneath it.

That's logical because the sediment making up that layer was deposited on top of, and therefore after, the layers below. So reading this diagram tells us basic information about the time that rock layers and rock units were formed relative to other layers.

Based on the radioactive clocks, we can conclude that these four rock units deep in the gorge (Table 1) are all older in a relative sense than the horizontal sedimentary layers in the Canyon walls. Conventionally the lowermost or oldest of these horizontal sedimentary layers is labeled early to middle Cambrian,[3] and thus regarded as about 510–520 million years old.[4] All the rocks below it are then labeled Precambrian and regarded as older than 542 million years.

So accordingly all four dated rock units (Table 1) are also Precambrian. And apart from the potassium-argon age for the Cardenas Basalt, all the radioactive clocks have correctly shown that these four rock units were formed earlier than Cambrian, so they are *pre*-Cambrian. (But the passage of time between these Precambrian rock units and the horizontal sedimentary layers above them was a maximum of about 1,700 years—the time between creation and the Flood—not millions of years.)

Similarly, in the relative sense the Brahma amphibolites and Elves Chasm Granodiorite are older (by hours or days) than the

Cardenas Basalt and Bass Rapids diabase sill (Figure 1). Once again, the radioactive clocks have correctly shown that those two rock units are older than the rock units above them.

Why then should we expect the radioactive clocks to yield relative ages that follow a logical pattern? (Actually, younger sedimentary layers yield a similar general pattern.[5]) The answer is again simple but profound! The radioactive clocks in the rock units at the bottom of the Grand Canyon, formed during Creation Week, have been ticking for longer than the radioactive clocks in the younger sedimentary layers higher up in the sequence that were formed later during the Flood.

Conclusion

Although it is a mistake to accept radioactive dates of millions of years, the clocks can still be useful to us, in principle, to date the relative sequence of rock formation during earth history.

The different clocks have ticked at different, faster rates in the past, so the standard old ages are certainly not accurate, correct, or absolute. However, because the radioactive clocks in rocks that formed early in earth history have been ticking longer, they should generally yield older radioactive ages than rock layers formed later.

So it is possible that relative radioactive ages of rocks, in addition to mineral contents and other rock features, could be used to compare and correlate similar rocks in other areas to find which ones formed at the same time during the events detailed in Genesis, God's eyewitness account of earth history.

1. T. Oberthür, D. W. Davis, T. G. Blenkinsop, and A. Höhndorf, "Precise U-Pb Mineral Ages, Rb-Sr and Sm-Nd Systematics of the Great Dyke, Zimbabwe—Constraints on Late Archean Events in the Zimbabwe Craton and Limpopo Belt," *Precambrian Research* 113:293–305, 2002; S. B. Mukasa, A. H. Wilson, and R. W. Carlson, "A Multielement Geochronologic Study of the Great Dyke, Zimbabwe: Significance of the Robust and Reset Ages," *Earth and Planetary Science Letters* 164:353–369, 1998; J. Zhao, and M. T. McCulloch, "Sm-Nd Mineral Isochron Ages of Late Proterozoic Dyke Swarms in Australia: Evidence for Two Distinctive Events of Mafic Magmatism and Crustal Extension," *Chemical Geology* 109:341–354, 1993.

2. A. A. Snelling, "Isochron Discordances and the Role of Inheritances and Mixing of Radioisotopes in the Mantle and Crust," in *Radioisotopes and the Age of the Earth: Results of a Young-Earth Creationist Research Initiative*, eds. L. Vardiman, A. A. Snelling, and E. F. Chaffin (El Cajon, California: Institute for Creation Research and Chino Valley, Arizona: Creation Research Society), pp. 393–524, 2005; D. B. DeYoung, "Radioisotope Dating Case Studies," in *Thousands . . . Not Billions* (Green Forest: Arkansas: Master Books), pp. 123–139, 2005.

3. L. K. Middleton and D. K. Elliott, "Tonto Group," in *Grand Canyon Geology*, 2nd ed., eds. S. S. Beus and M. Morales (New York: Oxford University Press), pp. 90–106, 2003.

4. F. M. Gradstein, J. G. Ogg, and A. G. Smith, eds., *A Geologic Time Scale 2004* (Cambridge University Press, United Kingdom), 2004.

5. J. Woodmorappe, "Radiometric Geochronology Appraised," *Creation Research Society Quarterly* 16:102–129, 147–148, 1979; D. R. Humphreys, "Accelerated Nuclear Decay: A Viable Hypothesis?" in *Radioisotopes and the Age of the Earth: A Young-Earth Creationist Research Initiative*, eds. L. Vardiman, A. A. Snelling, and E. F. Chaffin (El Cajon, California: Institute for Creation Research and St. Joseph, Missouri: Creation Research Society), pp. 333–379, 2000.

Doesn't Carbon-14 Dating Disprove the Bible?

by Mike Riddle

Scientists use a technique called radiometric dating to estimate the ages of rocks, fossils, and the earth. Many people have been led to believe that radiometric dating methods have proved the earth to be billions of years old. This has caused many in the church to reevaluate the biblical creation account, specifically the meaning of the word "day" in Genesis 1. With our focus on one particular form of radiometric dating—carbon dating—we will see that carbon dating strongly supports a young earth. Note that, contrary to a popular misconception, carbon dating is not used to date rocks at millions of years old.

Basics

Before we get into the details of how radiometric dating methods are used, we need to review some preliminary concepts from chemistry. Recall that atoms are the basic building blocks of matter. Atoms are made up of much smaller particles called protons, neutrons, and electrons. Protons and neutrons make up the center (nucleus) of the atom, and electrons form shells around the nucleus.

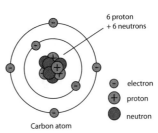

6 proton
+ 6 neutrons

electron
proton
neutron

Carbon atom

The number of protons in the nucleus of an atom determines the element. For example, all carbon atoms have 6 protons, all atoms of nitrogen have 7 protons, and all oxygen atoms have 8 protons. The number of neutrons in the nucleus can vary in any given type of atom. So, a carbon atom might have six neutrons, or seven, or possibly eight—but it would always have six protons. An "isotope" is any of several different forms of an element, each having different numbers of neutrons. The illustration below shows the three isotopes of carbon.

Some isotopes of certain elements are unstable; they can spontaneously change into another kind of atom in a process called "radioactive decay." Since this process presently happens at a known measured rate, scientists attempt to use it like a "clock" to tell how long ago a rock or fossil formed. There are two main applications for radiometric dating. One is for potentially dating fossils (once-living things) using carbon-14 dating, and the other is for dating rocks and the age of the earth using uranium, potassium, and other radioactive atoms.

The atomic number corresponds to the number of protons in an atom. Atomic mass is a combination of the number of protons and neutrons in the nucleus. (The electrons are so much lighter that they do not contribute significantly to the mass of an atom.)

Carbon-14 dating

Carbon-14 (^{14}C), also referred to as radiocarbon, is claimed to be a reliable dating method for determining the ages of fossils up to 50,000 to 60,000 years. If this claim is true, the biblical account of a young earth (about 6,000 years) is in question, since ^{14}C dates of tens of thousands of years are common.[1]

When a scientist's interpretation of data does not match the clear meaning of the text in the Bible, we should never reinterpret the Bible. God knows just what He meant to say, and His understanding of science is infallible, whereas ours is fallible. So we should never think it necessary to modify His Word. Genesis 1 defines the days of creation to be literal days (a number with the word "day" always means a normal day in the Old Testament, and the phrase "evening and morning" further defines the days as literal days). Since the Bible is the inspired Word of God, we should examine the validity of the standard interpretation of ^{14}C dating by asking several questions:

1. Is the explanation of the data derived from empirical, observational science, or an interpretation of past events (historical science)?

2. Are there any assumptions involved in the dating method?

3. Are the dates provided by ^{14}C dating consistent with what we observe?

4. Do all scientists accept the ^{14}C dating method as reliable and accurate?

All radiometric dating methods use scientific procedures in the present to interpret what has happened in the past. The procedures used are not necessarily in question. The interpretation of past events is in question. The secular (evolutionary) worldview interprets the universe and world to be billions of years old. The Bible teaches a young universe and earth. Which worldview does science support? Can carbon-14 dating help solve the mystery of which worldview is more accurate?

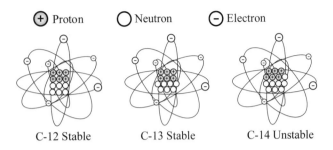

| $\oplus$ Proton | $\bigcirc$ Neutron | $\ominus$ Electron |

C-12 Stable   C-13 Stable   C-14 Unstable

The use of carbon-14 dating is often misunderstood. Carbon-14 is mostly used to date once-living things (organic material). It cannot be used directly to date rocks; however, it can potentially be used to put time constraints on some inorganic material such as diamonds (diamonds could contain carbon-14). Because of the rapid rate of decay of ^{14}C, it can only give dates in the thousands-of-year range and not millions.

There are three different naturally occurring varieties (isotopes) of carbon: ^{12}C, ^{13}C, and ^{14}C.

Carbon-14 is used for dating because it is unstable (radioactive), whereas ^{12}C and ^{13}C are stable. Radioactive means that ^{14}C will decay (emit radiation) over time and become a different element. During this process (called "beta decay") a neutron in the ^{14}C atom will be converted into a proton. By losing one neutron and gaining one proton, ^{14}C is changed into nitrogen-14 (^{14}N = 7 protons and 7 neutrons).

If ^{14}C is constantly decaying, will the earth eventually run out of ^{14}C? The answer is no. Carbon-14 is constantly being added to the atmosphere. Cosmic rays from outer space, which contain high levels of energy, bombard the earth's upper atmosphere. These cosmic rays collide with atoms in the atmosphere and can cause them to come apart. Neutrons that come from these fragmented atoms collide with ^{14}N atoms (the atmosphere is made mostly of nitrogen and oxygen) and convert them into ^{14}C atoms (a proton changes into a neutron).

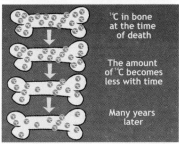

^{14}C in bone at the time of death

The amount of ^{14}C becomes less with time

Many years later

Once ^{14}C is produced, it combines with oxygen in the atmosphere (^{12}C behaves like ^{14}C and also combines with oxygen) to

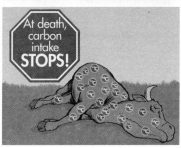

At death, carbon intake STOPS!

form carbon dioxide (CO^2). Because CO_2 gets incorporated into plants (which means the food we eat contains ^{14}C and ^{12}C), all living things should have the same ratio of ^{14}C and ^{12}C in them as in the air we breathe.

How the carbon-14 dating process works

Once a living thing dies, the dating process begins. As long as an organism is alive it will continue to take in ^{14}C; however, when it dies, it will stop. Since ^{14}C is radioactive (decays into

^{14}N), the amount of ^{14}C in a dead organism gets less and less over time. Therefore, part of the dating process involves measuring the amount of ^{14}C that remains after some has been lost (decayed). Scientists now use a device called an "Accelerator Mass Spectrometer" (AMS) to determine the ratio of ^{14}C to ^{12}C, which increases the assumed accuracy to about 80,000 years. In order to actually do the dating, other things need to be known. Two such things include the following questions:

1. How fast does ^{14}C decay?

2. What was the starting amount of ^{14}C in the creature when it died?

The decay rate of radioactive elements is described in terms of half-life. The half-life of an atom is the amount of time it takes for half of the atoms in a sample to decay. The half-life of ^{14}C is 5,730 years. For example, a jar starting full of ^{14}C atoms at time zero will contain half ^{14}C atoms and half ^{14}N atoms at the end of 5,730 years (one half-life). At the end of 11,460 years (two half-lives) the jar will contain one-quarter ^{14}C atoms and three-quarter ^{14}N atoms.

Since the half-life of ^{14}C is known (how fast it decays), the only part left to determine is the starting amount of ^{14}C in a fossil. If scientists know the original amount of ^{14}C in a creature when it died, they can measure the current amount and then calculate how many half-lives have passed.

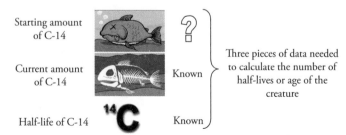

Starting amount of C-14

Current amount of C-14 — Known

Half-life of C-14 — Known

Three pieces of data needed to calculate the number of half-lives or age of the creature

Since no one was there to measure the amount of ^{14}C when a creature died, scientists need to find a method to determine how much ^{14}C has decayed. To do this, scientists use the main isotope of carbon, called carbon-12 (^{12}C). Because ^{12}C is a stable isotope of carbon, it will remain constant; however, the amount of ^{14}C will decrease after a creature dies. All living things take in carbon (^{14}C and ^{12}C) from eating and breathing. Therefore, the ratio of ^{14}C to ^{12}C in living creatures will be the same as in the atmosphere. This ratio turns out to be about one ^{14}C atom for every 1 trillion ^{12}C atoms. Scientists can use this ratio to help determine the starting amount of ^{14}C.

When an organism dies, this ratio (1 to 1 trillion) will begin to change. The amount of ^{12}C will remain constant, but the amount of ^{14}C will become less and less. The smaller the ratio, the longer the organism has been dead. The following illustration demonstrates how the age is estimated using this ratio.

Percent ^{14}C Remaining	Percent ^{12}C Remaining	Ratio	Number of Half-Lives	Years Dead (Age of Fossil)
100	100	1 to 1T	0	0
50	100	1 to 2T	1	5,730
25	100	1 to 4T	2	11,460
12.5	100	1 to 8T	3	17,190
6.25	100	1 to 16T	4	22,920
3.125	100	1 to 32T	5	28,650

T = Trillion

A critical assumption

A critical assumption used in carbon-14 dating has to do with this ratio. It is assumed that the ratio of ^{14}C to ^{12}C in the atmosphere has always been the same as it is today (1 to 1 trillion). If this assumption is true, then the AMS ^{14}C dating method is valid up to about 80,000 years. Beyond this number, the instruments scientists use would not be able to detect enough remaining ^{14}C to be useful in age estimates. This is a critical assumption in the dating process. If this assumption is not true, then the method will give incorrect dates. What could cause this ratio to change? If the production rate of ^{14}C in the atmosphere is not equal to the removal rate (mostly through decay), this ratio will change. In other words, the amount of ^{14}C being produced in the atmosphere must equal the amount being removed to be in a steady state (also called "equilibrium"). If this is not true, the ratio of ^{14}C to ^{12}C is not a constant, which would make knowing the starting amount of ^{14}C in a specimen difficult or impossible to accurately determine.

Dr. Willard Libby, the founder of the carbon-14 dating method, assumed this ratio to be constant. His reasoning was based on a belief in evolution, which assumes the earth must be billions of years old. Assumptions in the scientific community are extremely important. If the starting assumption is false, all the calculations based on that assumption might be correct but still give a wrong conclusion.

In Dr. Libby's original work, he noted that the atmosphere did not appear to be in equilibrium. This was a troubling idea for Dr. Libby since he believed the world was billions of years old and enough time had passed to achieve equilibrium. Dr. Libby's calculations showed that if the earth started with no ^{14}C in the atmosphere, it would take up to 30,000 years to build up to a steady state (equilibrium).

If the cosmic radiation has remained at its present intensity for 20,000 or 30,000 years, and if the carbon reservoir has not changed appreciably in this time, then there exists at the present time a complete balance between the rate of disintegration of radiocarbon atoms and the rate of assimilation of new radiocarbon atoms for all material in the life-cycle.[2]

Dr. Libby chose to ignore this discrepancy (nonequilibrium state), and he attributed it to experimental error. However, the discrepancy has turned out to be very real. The ratio of $^{14}C / ^{12}C$ is not constant.

The Specific Production Rate (SPR) of ^{14}C is known to be 18.8 atoms per gram of total carbon per minute. The Specific

Decay Rate (SDR) is known to be only 16.1 disintegrations per gram per minute.[3]

What does this mean? If it takes about 30,000 years to reach equilibrium and ^{14}C is still out of equilibrium, then maybe the earth is not very old.

Magnetic field of the earth

Other factors can affect the production rate of ^{14}C in the atmosphere. The earth has a magnetic field around it which helps protect us from harmful radiation from outer space. This magnetic field is decaying (getting weaker). The stronger the field is around the earth, the fewer the number of cosmic rays that are able to reach the atmosphere. This would result in a smaller production of ^{14}C in the atmosphere in earth's past.

> The cause for the long term variation of the C-14 level is not known. The variation is certainly partially the result of a change in the cosmic ray production rate of radiocarbon. The cosmic-ray flux, and hence the production rate of C-14, is a function not only of the solar activity but also of the magnetic dipole moment of the earth.[4]

> Though complex, this history of the earth's magnetic field agrees with Barnes' basic hypothesis, that the field has always freely decayed. . . . The field has always been losing energy despite its variations, so it cannot be more than 10,000 years old.[5]

Earth's magnetic field is fading. Today it is about 10 percent weaker than it was when German mathematician Carl Friedrich Gauss started keeping tabs on it in 1845, scientists say.[6]

If the production rate of ^{14}C in the atmosphere was less in the past, dates given using the carbon-14 method would incorrectly assume that more ^{14}C had decayed out of a specimen than what has actually occurred. This would result in giving older dates than the true age.

Genesis Flood

What role might the Genesis Flood have played in the amount of carbon? The Flood would have buried large amounts of carbon from living organisms (plant and animal) to form today's fossil fuels (coal, oil, etc.). The amount of fossil fuels indicates there must have been a vastly larger quantity of vegetation in existence prior to the Flood than exists today. This means that the biosphere just prior to the Flood might have had 500 times more carbon in living organisms than today. This would further dilute the amount of ^{14}C and cause the $^{14}C/^{12}C$ ratio to be much smaller than today.

> If that were the case, and this C-14 were distributed uniformly throughout the biosphere, and the total amount of biosphere C were, for example, 500 times that of today's world, the resulting C-14/C-12 ratio would be 1/500 of today's level . . . .[7]

When the Flood is taken into account, along with the decay of the magnetic field, it is reasonable to believe that the assumption of equilibrium is a false assumption.

Because of this false assumption, any age estimates using ^{14}C on organic material that dates from prior to the Flood will give much older dates than the true ages. Pre-Flood organic materials would be dated at perhaps ten times the true age.

The RATE group findings

In 1997 an eight-year research project was started to investigate the age of the earth. The group was called the RATE group (Radioisotopes and the Age of The Earth). The team of scientists included:

- Larry Vardiman, PhD Atmospheric Science

- Russell Humphreys, PhD Physics

- Eugene Chaffin, PhD Physics

- Donald DeYoung, PhD Physics

- John Baumgardner, PhD Geophysics

- Steven Austin, PhD Geology

- Andrew Snelling, PhD Geology

- Steven Boyd, PhD Hebraic and Cognate Studies

The objective was to gather data commonly ignored or censored by evolutionary standards of dating. The scientists reviewed the assumptions and procedures used in estimating the ages of rocks and fossils. The results of the carbon-14 dating demonstrated serious problems for long geologic ages. For example, a series of fossilized wood samples that conventionally have been dated according to their host strata to be from Tertiary to Permian (40–250 million years old) all yielded significant, detectable levels of carbon-14 that would conventionally equate to only 30,000–45,000 years "ages" for the original trees.[8] Similarly, a survey of the conventional radiocarbon journals resulted in more than forty examples of supposedly ancient organic materials, including limestones, that contained carbon-14, as reported by leading laboratories.[9]

Samples were then taken from ten different coal layers that, according to evolutionists, represent different time periods in the geologic column (Cenozoic, Mesozoic, and Paleozoic). The RATE group obtained these ten coal samples from the U.S. Department of Energy Coal Sample Bank, from samples collected from major coalfields across the United States. The chosen coal samples, which dated millions to hundreds of millions of years old based on standard evolution time estimates, all contained measurable amounts of ^{14}C. In all cases, careful precautions were taken to eliminate any possibility of contamination from other sources. Samples, in all three "time periods," displayed significant amounts of ^{14}C. This is a significant discovery. Since the half-life of ^{14}C is relatively short (5,730 years), there should be no detectable ^{14}C left after about

100,000 years. The average ^{14}C estimated age for all the layers from these three time periods was approximately 50,000 years. However, using a more realistic pre-Flood $^{14}C/^{12}C$ ratio reduces that age to about 5,000 years.

These results indicate that the entire fossil-bearing geologic column is much less than 100,000 years old—and even much younger. This confirms the Bible and challenges the evolutionary idea of long geologic ages.

> Because the lifetime of C-14 is so brief, these AMS [Accelerator Mass Spectrometer] measurements pose an obvious challenge to the standard geological timescale that assigns millions to hundreds of millions of years to this part of the rock layer.[10]

Another noteworthy observation from the RATE group was the amount of ^{14}C found in diamonds. Secular scientists have estimated the ages of diamonds to be millions to billions of years old using other radiometric dating methods. These methods are also based on questionable assumptions and are discussed elsewhere.[11] Because of their hardness, diamonds (the hardest known substance) are extremely resistant to contamination through chemical exchange. Since diamonds are considered to be so old by evolutionary standards, finding any ^{14}C in them would be strong support for a recent creation.

The RATE group analyzed twelve diamond samples for possible carbon-14 content. Similar to the coal results, all twelve diamond samples contained detectable, but lower levels of ^{14}C. These findings are powerful evidence that coal and diamonds cannot be the millions or billions of years old that evolutionists claim. Indeed, these RATE findings of detectable ^{14}C in diamonds have been confirmed independently.[12] Carbon-14 found in fossils at all layers of the geologic column, in coal and in diamonds, is evidence which confirms the biblical timescale of thousands of years and not billions.

> Because of C-14's short half-life, such a finding would argue that carbon and probably the entire physical earth as well must have a recent origin.[13]

Conclusion

All radiometric dating methods are based on assumptions about events that happened in the past. If the assumptions are accepted as true (as is typically done in the evolutionary dating processes), results can be biased toward a desired age. In the reported ages given in textbooks and other journals, these evolutionary assumptions have not been questioned, while results inconsistent with long ages have been censored. When the assumptions are evaluated and shown to be faulty, the results support the biblical account of a global Flood and young earth. Thus, Christians should not be afraid of radiometric dating methods. Carbon-14 dating is really the friend of Christians because it supports a young earth.

The RATE scientists are convinced that the popular idea attributed to geologist Charles Lyell from nearly two centuries ago, "The present is the key to the past," is simply not valid for an earth history of millions or billions of years. An alternative interpretation of the carbon-14 data is that the earth experienced a global flood catastrophe which laid down most of the rock strata and fossils. . . . Whatever the source of the carbon-14, its presence in nearly every sample tested worldwide is a strong challenge to an ancient age. Carbon-14 data is now firmly on the side of the young-earth view of history.[14]

1. *Earth Science,* Teachers Edition (Upper Saddle River, New Jersey: Prentice Hall, 2002), p. 301.

2. W. Libby, *Radiocarbon Dating* (Chicago: Univ. of Chicago Press, 1952), p. 8.

3. C. Sewell, "Carbon-14 and the age of the earth," online at www.rae.org/bits23.htm.

4. M. Stuiver and H. Suess, "On the relationship between radiocarbon dates and true sample ages," *Radiocarbon* 8:1966, 535.

5. R. Humphreys, "The mystery of earth's magnetic field," *ICR Impact #292*, Feb 1, 1989, online at www.icr.org/article/292.

6. J. Roach, *National Geographic News*, September 9, 2004.

7. J. Baumgardner, "C-14 evidence for a recent global Flood and a young earth" in L. Vardiman, A.A. Snelling, and E.F. Chaffin (Eds.), *Radioisotopes and the Age of the Earth, Vol. 2* (Santee, California: Institute for Creation Research, 2005), p. 618.

8. A.A. Snelling, "Radioactive 'dating' in conflict! Fossil wood in ancient lava flow yields radiocarbon," *Creation Ex Nihilo* 20 no. 1 (1997):24–27; A.A. Snelling, "Stumping old-age dogma: radiocarbon in an 'ancient' fossil tree stump casts doubt on traditional rock/fossil dating," *Creation Ex Nihilo* 20 no. 4 (1998):48–51; A.A. Snelling, "Dating dilemma: fossil wood in ancient sandstone," *Creation Ex Nihilo* 21 no. 3 (1992):39–41; A.A. Snelling, "Geological conflict: young radiocarbon date for ancient fossil wood challenges fossil dating," *Creation Ex Nihilo* 22 no. 2 (2000):44–47; A.A. Snelling, "Conflicting 'ages' of Tertiary basalt and contained fossilized wood, Crinum, central Queensland, Australia," *Creation Ex Nihilo* 14 no. 2 (2000):99–122.

9. P. Giem, "Carbon-14 content of fossil carbon," *Origins* 51 (2001):6–30.

10. J.R. Baumgardner, ibid., p. 587.

11. M. Riddle,"Does radiometric dating prove the earth is old?" in K.A. Ham (Ed.), *The New Answers Book 1* (Green Forest, Arkansas: Master Books, 2006), pp. 113–124.

12. R.E. Taylor and J. Southon, "Use of natural diamonds to monitor ^{14}C AMS instrument grounds," *Nuclear Instruments and Methods in Physics Research B* 259 (2007):282–287.

13. J.R. Baumgardner, ibid., p. 609.

14. D. DeYoung, *Thousands . . . Not Billions* (Green Forest, Arkansas: Master Books, 2005), p. 61.

Mike Riddle, a former captain in the U.S. Marine Corps, is a well-known creation speaker for Answers in Genesis–USA. He holds a bachelors degree in mathematics and a masters in education. Mike was also a U.S. national track-and-field pentathlon champion.

Where Did the Idea of "Millions of Years" Come From?

by Terry Mortenson

Today, most people in the world, including most people in the church, take for granted that the earth and universe are millions and millions (even billions) of years old. Our public schools, from kindergarten on up, teach these vast ages, and one is scoffed at if he questions them. But it has not always been that way, and it is important to understand how this change took place and why.

Geology's early beginnings

Geology as a separate field of science with systematic field studies, collection and classification of rocks and fossils, and development of theoretical reconstructions of the historical events that formed those rock layers and fossils, is only about 200 years old. Prior to this, back to ancient Greek times, people had noticed fossils in the rocks. Many believed that the fossils were the remains of former living things turned to stone, and many early Christians (including Tertullian, Chrysostom, and Augustine) attributed them to Noah's Flood. But others rejected these ideas and regarded fossils as either jokes of nature, the products of rocks endowed with life in some sense, the creative works of God, or perhaps even the deceptions of Satan. The debate was finally settled when Robert Hooke (1635–1703) confirmed by microscopic analysis of fossil wood that fossils were the mineralized remains of former living creatures.

We will see that science does not require millions of years, but rather it is a necessity of uniformitarian geology and evolutionary theory.

Prior to 1750 one of the most important geological thinkers was Niels Steensen (1638–1686), or Steno, a Dutch anatomist and geologist. He established the principle of superposition, namely that sedimentary rock layers are deposited in a successive, essentially horizontal fashion, so that a lower stratum was deposited before the one above it. In his book *Forerunner* (1669) he expressed belief in a roughly 6,000-year-old earth and that fossil-bearing rock strata were deposited by Noah's Flood. Over the next century, several authors, including the English geologist John Woodward (1665–1722) and the German geologist Johann Lehmann (1719–1767), wrote books essentially reinforcing that view.

In the latter decades of the 18th century, some French and Italian geologists rejected the biblical account of the Flood and attributed the rock record to natural processes occurring over a long period of time. Several prominent Frenchmen also contributed to the idea of millions of years. The widely respected scientist Comte de Buffon (1707–1788) imagined in his book *Epochs of Nature* (1779) that the earth was once like a hot molten ball that had cooled to reach its present state over about 75,000 years (though his unpublished manuscript says about 3,000,000 years). The astronomer Pierre Laplace (1749–1827) proposed the nebular hypothesis in his *Exposition of the System of the Universe* (1796). This theory said that the solar system was once a hot, spinning gas cloud, which over long ages gradually cooled and condensed to form the planets. Jean Lamarck, a specialist in shell creatures, advocated a theory of biological evolution over long ages in his *Philosophy of Zoology* (1809).

Abraham Werner (1749–1817) was a popular mineralogy professor in Germany. He believed that most of the crust of the earth had been precipitated chemically or mechanically by a slowly receding global ocean over the course of about a million years. It was an elegantly simple theory, but Werner failed to take into account the fossils in the rocks. This was a serious mistake since the fossils tell much about when and how quickly the sediments were deposited and transformed into stone. Many of the greatest geologists of the 19th century were Werner's students, who were impacted by his idea of a very long history for the earth.

In Scotland, James Hutton (1726–1797) was developing a different theory of earth history. He studied medicine at the university. After his studies he took over the family farm for a while. But he soon discovered his real love: the study of the earth. In 1788 he published a journal article and in 1795 a book, both by the title *Theory of the Earth*. He proposed that the continents were being slowly eroded into the oceans. Those sediments were gradually hardened by the internal heat of the earth and then raised by convulsions to become new landmasses, which would later be eroded into the oceans, hardened and elevated. So in his view, earth history was cyclical; and he stated that he could find no evidence of a beginning in the rock record, making earth history indefinitely long.

Catastrophist—Uniformitarian debate

Neither Werner nor Hutton paid much attention to the fossils. However, in the early 1800s Georges Cuvier (1768–1832), the famous French comparative anatomist and vertebrate palaeontologist, developed his *catastrophist* theory of earth history. It was expressed most clearly in his *Discourse on the Revolutions of the Surface of the Globe* (1812). Cuvier believed that over the course of long, untold ages of earth history, many catastrophic floods of regional or nearly global extent had destroyed and buried creatures in sediments. All but one of these catastrophes occurred before the creation of man.

Georges Cuvier (1768–1832)

Charles Lyell (1797–1875)

William Smith (1769–1839) was a drainage engineer and surveyor, who in the course of his work around Great Britain became fascinated with the strata and fossils. Like Cuvier, he had an old-earth catastrophist view of earth history. In three works published from 1815 to 1817, he presented the first geological map of England and Wales and explained an order and relative chronology of the rock formations as defined by certain characteristic (index) fossils. He became known as the "Father of English Stratigraphy" because he developed the method of giving relative dates to the rock layers on the basis of the fossils found in them.

A massive blow to catastrophism came during the years 1830 to 1833, when Charles Lyell (1797–1875), a lawyer and former student of Buckland, published his influential three-volume work *Principles of Geology*. Reviving and augmenting the ideas of Hutton, Lyell's *Principles* set forth the principles by which he thought geological interpretations should be made. His theory was a radical *uniformitarianism* in which he insisted that only present-day processes of geological change at *present-day rates of intensity and magnitude* should be used to interpret the rock record of past geological activity. In other words, geological processes of change have been uniform throughout earth history. No continental or global catastrophic floods have ever occurred, insisted Lyell.

Lyell is often given too much credit (or blame) for destroying faith in the Genesis Flood and the biblical timescale. But we must realize that many Christians (geologists and theologians) contributed to this undermining of biblical teaching before Lyell's book appeared. Although the catastrophist theory had greatly reduced the geological significance of Noah's Flood and expanded earth history well beyond the traditional biblical view, Lyell's work was the final blow for belief in the Flood. By explaining the whole rock record by slow gradual processes, he thereby reduced the Flood to a geological nonevent. Catastrophism did not die out immediately, although by the late 1830s only a few catastrophists remained, and they believed Noah's Flood was geologically insignificant.

By the end of the 19th century, the age of the earth was considered by all geologists to be in the hundreds of millions of years. Radiometric dating methods began to be developed in 1903, and over the course of the 20th century the age of the earth expanded to 4.5 billion years.

Christian responses to old-earth geology

During the first half of the nineteenth century the church responded in various ways to these old-earth theories of the catastrophists and uniformitarians. A number of writers in Great Britain (and a few in America), who became known as "scriptural geologists," raised biblical, geological, and philosophical arguments against the old-earth theories. Some of them were scientists, some were clergy. Some were both ordained and scientifically well informed, as was common in those days. Many of them were very geologically competent by the standards of their day, both by reading and by their own careful observations of rocks and fossils. They believed that the biblical account of Creation and

Genesis 1:1
In the beginning God created the heaven and the earth.

THE GAP?
- Millions or billions of years
- Geologic ages
- Lucifer's Flood

Genesis 1:2
And the earth was without form, and void; and darkness was upon the face of the deep. And the Spirit of God moved upon the face of the waters.

Noah's Flood explained the rock record far better than the old-earth theories.[1]

Other Christians in the early 1800s quickly accepted the idea of millions of years and tried to fit all this time into Genesis, even though the uniformitarians and catastrophists were still debating and geology was in its infancy as a science. In 1804 Thomas Chalmers (1780–1847), a young Presbyterian pastor, began to preach that Christians should accept the millions of years; and in an 1814 review of Cuvier's book, he proposed that all the time could fit between Genesis 1:1 and 1:2. By that time Chalmers was becoming a highly influential evangelical leader and, consequently, this "gap theory" became very popular. In 1823 the respected Anglican theologian George Stanley Faber (1773–1854) began to advocate the day-age view, namely that the days of creation were not literal but figurative for long ages.

To accept these geological ages, Christians also had to reinterpret the Flood. In the 1820s John Fleming (1785–1857), a Presbyterian minister, contended that Noah's Flood was so peaceful it left no lasting geological evidence. John Pye Smith (1774–1851), a Congregational theologian, preferred to see it as a localized inundation in the Mesopotamian valley (modern-day Iraq).

Liberal theology, which by the early 1800s was dominating the church in Europe, was beginning to make inroads into Britain and North America in the 1820s. The liberals considered Genesis 1–11 to be as historically unreliable and unscientific as the creation and flood myths of the ancient Babylonians, Sumerians, and Egyptians.

In spite of the efforts of the scriptural geologists, these various old-earth reinterpretations of Genesis prevailed so that by 1845 all the commentaries on Genesis had abandoned the biblical chronology and the global Flood; and by the time of Darwin's *Origin of Species* (1859), the young-earth view had essentially disappeared within the church. From that time onward, most Christian leaders and scholars of the church accepted the millions of years and insisted that the age of the earth was not important. Many godly men also soon accepted evolution as well. Space allows only mention of a few examples.

The Baptist "prince of preachers" Charles Spurgeon (1834–1892) uncritically accepted the old-earth geological theory (though he never explained how to fit the long ages into the Bible). In an 1855 sermon he said,

Can any man tell me when the beginning was? Years ago we thought the beginning of this world was when Adam came upon it; but we have discovered that thousands of years before that God was preparing chaotic matter to make it a fit abode for man, putting races of creatures upon it, who might die and leave behind the marks of his handiwork and marvelous skill, before he tried his hand on man.[2]

The great Presbyterian theologian at Princeton Seminary Charles Hodge (1779–1878) insisted that the age of the earth was not important. He favored the gap theory initially and switched to the day-age view later in life. His compromise contributed to the eventual victory of liberal theology at Princeton about 50 years after his death.[3]

C. I. Scofield put the gap theory in notes on Genesis 1:2 in his Scofield Reference Bible, which was used by millions of Christians around the world. More recently, a respected Old Testament scholar reasoned,

> From a superficial reading of Genesis 1, the impression would seem to be that the entire creative process took place in six twenty-four-hour days. If this was the true intent of the Hebrew author . . . this seems to run counter to modern scientific research, which indicates that the planet Earth was created several billion years ago . . . .[4]

Numerous similar statements from Christian scholars and leaders in the last few decades could be quoted to show that their interpretation of Genesis is controlled by the fact that they assume that geologists have proven millions of years. As a result, most seminaries and Christian colleges around the world are compromised.

Compromise unnecessary

The sad irony of all this compromise is that in the last half century, the truth of Genesis 1–11 has been increasingly vindicated, often unintentionally by the work of evolutionists. Lyell's uniformitarian *Principles* dominated geology until about the 1970s, when Derek Ager (1923–1993), a prominent British geologist, and others increasingly challenged Lyell's assumptions and argued that much of the rock record shows evidence of rapid catastrophic erosion or sedimentation, drastically reducing the time involved in the formation of many geological deposits. Ager, an atheist to his death (as far as one can tell from his writings), explained the influence of Lyell on geology this way:

> My excuse for this lengthy and amateur digression into history is that I have been trying to show how I think geology got into the hands of the theoreticians [uniformitarians] who were conditioned by the social and political history of their day more than by observations in the field. . . . In other words, we have allowed ourselves to be brain-washed into avoiding any interpretation of the past that involves extreme and what might be termed "catastrophic" processes.[5]

These "neocatastrophist" reinterpretations of the rocks have developed contemporaneously with a resurgence of "Flood geology," a view of earth history very similar to that of the 19th century scriptural geologists and a key ingredient of young-earth creationism, which was essentially launched into the world by the publication of *The Genesis Flood* (1961) by Drs. John Whitcomb and Henry Morris. This movement is now worldwide in scope, and the scientific sophistication of the scientific model is rapidly increasing with time.

Many Christians today are arguing that we need to contend against Darwinism with "intelligent design" arguments and leave Genesis out of the public discussion. But this strategy was tried in the early 19th century with many writings on natural theology, culminating in the famous eight volumes of the 1830s that collectively became known as the *Bridgewater Treatises*. These books were "preaching to the choir" and did nothing to retard the slide in the culture toward atheism and deism. In fact, by compromising on the age of the earth and ignoring Scripture in their defense of Christianity, they actually contributed to the weakening of the church. The same is happening today.

The renowned atheist evolutionist and Harvard University biologist Ernst Mayr said this:

> The [Darwinian] revolution began when it became obvious that the earth was very ancient rather than having been created only 6000 years ago. This finding was the snowball that started the whole avalanche.[6]

Mayr was right about the age of the earth (not Darwin's theory) being the beginning of the avalanche of unbelief. He was wrong that the idea of millions of years was a "finding" of scientific research. Rather, it was the fruit of antibiblical philosophical assumptions used to interpret the rocks and fossils. Historical research has shown that Laplace was an open atheist, that Buffon, Lamarck, Werner, and Hutton were deists or atheists, and that Cuvier, William Smith, and Lyell were deists or vague theists. These men (who influenced the thinking of compromised Christians) were NOT unbiased objective pursuers of truth.

Typical of what Lyell, Buffon, and others wrote is Hutton's statement. He insisted, "The past history of our globe must be explained by what can be seen to be happening now. . . . No powers are to be employed that are not natural to the globe, no action to be admitted except those of which we know the principle."[7] By insisting that geologists must reason only from known, present-day natural processes, Hutton ruled out supernatural creation and the unique global Flood of Genesis, before he ever looked at the rocks.

Disastrous consequences of compromise

The scriptural geologists of the early 19th century opposed old-earth geological theories not only because the theories reflected erroneous scientific reasoning and were contrary to Scripture, but also because they believed that Christian compromise with such theories would eventually have a catastrophic effect on the health of the church and her witness to a lost world. Henry Cole, an Anglican minister, wrote:

> Many reverend geologists, however, would evince their reverence for the divine Revelation by making a distinction between its *historical* and its *moral* portions; and maintaining, that the latter only is inspired and absolute Truth; but that the former is not so; and therefore is open to any latitude of philosophic and scientific interpretation, modification or denial! According to these impious and infidel modifiers and separators, there is not one third of the Word of God that *is* inspired; for not more, nor perhaps so much, of that Word, is occupied in abstract moral revelation,

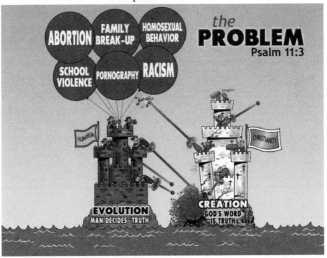

instruction, and precept. The other two thirds, therefore, are open to any scientific modification and interpretation; or, (if scientifically required,) to a total denial! It may however be safely asserted, that whoever professedly, before men, disbelieves the inspiration of any part of Revelation, disbelieves, in the sight of God, its inspiration altogether. . . . What the consequences of such things must be to a revelation-possessing land, time will rapidly and awfully unfold in its opening pages of national skepticism, infidelity, and apostasy, and of God's righteous vengeance on the same![8]

Cole and other opponents of the old-earth theories rightly understood that the historical portions of the Bible (including Genesis 1–11) are foundational to the theological and moral teachings of Scripture. Destroy the credibility of the former and sooner or later you will see rejection of the latter both inside and outside the church. If the scriptural geologists were alive today and saw the castle diagram shown below, they would say, "That pictures exactly what we were concerned about!" The history of the once-Christian nations in Europe and North America has confirmed the scriptural geologists' worst fears about the church and society.

It is time for the church, especially her leaders and scholars, to stop ignoring the age of the earth and the scientific evidence that increasingly vindicates the Word of God. The church must repent of her compromise with millions of years and once again believe and preach the literal truth of Genesis 1–11. It is time to take the church back to Genesis.

1. See T. Mortenson, *The Great Turning Point: The Church's Catastrophic Mistake on Geology—Before Darwin* (Green Forest, Arkansas: Master Books, 2004) for a full discussion of these men and the battle they fought against these developing old-earth theories and Christian compromises.

2. C.H. Spurgeon, "Election," *The New Park Street Pulpit* 1 (1990): 318.

3. See J. Pipa and D. Hall (Eds.), *Did God Create in Six Days?* (White Hall, West Virginia: Tolle Lege Press, 2005), pp. 7–16, for some of the documentation of this sad slide into apostasy.

4. G. Archer, *A Survey of Old Testament Introduction* (Chicago: Moody Publishers, 1985), p. 187.

5. D. Ager, *The Nature of the Stratigraphical Record* (London: Macmillan Press, 1981), pp. 46–47.

6. E. Mayr, "The nature of the Darwinian revolution," *Science* 176 (1972):988.

7. J. Hutton, "Theory of the Earth," *Trans. of the Royal Society of Edinburgh* vol. 1, part 2 (1788), quoted in A. Holmes, *Principles of Physical Geology* (New York: Ronald Press Co.,1965), pp. 43–44.

8. H. Cole, *Popular Geology Subversive of Divine Revelation* (London: Hatchard and Son, 1834), pp. ix–x, 44–45 footnote.

Terry Mortenson earned a PhD in the history of geology from the University of Coventry in England and an MDiv from Trinity Evangelical Divinity School in Chicago. Dr. Mortenson has lectured on the creation-evolution controversy in 19 countries since the late 1970s. He has also participated in seven formal debates with PhD evolutionary scientists in secular venues in four countries.

Dr. Mortenson is the author of numerous magazine, journal, and web articles, as well as several book chapters. The revised version of his PhD thesis was published as *The Great Turning Point: the Church's Catastrophic Mistake on Geology—Before Darwin*. Dr. Mortenson co-edited and contributed two chapters to the scholarly 14-author book *Coming to Grips with Genesis: Biblical Authority and the Age of the Earth*. Currently he serves as a speaker, researcher, and writer for Answers in Genesis–USA.

Raising the Bar on Creation Research

by Don DeYoung

One essential component of evolution is an extremely long timescale for earth history. Multibillions of years likewise are required by the big bang theory. However, this assumption of unlimited time is strongly challenged by recent creation research. From 1997 to 2005 a team of creation scientists explored the centerpiece of geologic time—radioisotope dating. This technique, developed over the last century, is used to date thousands of rocks, fossils and artifacts. The creation research project was given the acronym RATE, which stands for Radioisotopes and the Age of The Earth. Rock and mineral samples were collected from around the world and then dated by top laboratories. The RATE results conflict with geologic time and instead support a recent creation.

Carbon-14

Carbon-14 (^{14}C) is by far the most familiar radioisotope dating method. There is a common misconception that ^{14}C supports an ancient age for the earth. This is not the case, however, because ^{14}C has a short half-life compared with other dating isotopes—"just" 5,730 years. Carbon-14 is limited to dating objects thousands of years old, but not millions or billions of years. For samples that are truly ancient, any initial ^{14}C content should have completely decayed away.

And here arises a major challenge to a long timescale: in recent years, carbon-14 atoms have been found in samples of rocks, fossils, coal, and oil, which are thought to be very old. The RATE research team explored this anomaly with new measurements of ^{14}C in ten distinct coal samples. These coals are traditionally dated at 34–311 million years old. With utmost care to avoid contamination, traces of carbon-14 were found in all ten samples.

The pervasive presence of carbon-14 in earth materials supports biblical creation.

The RATE team next sought a more extreme challenge to age assumptions. Twelve diamond samples were obtained and prepared for ^{14}C analysis. Such measurements had not been previously reported because diamonds are assumed to be at least a billion years old and therefore entirely free of ^{14}C. Similar to the coal results, however, carbon-14 atoms were found in every diamond tested. The conclusion is clear: carbon-14 atoms in coal, diamonds, and a host of other materials provide strong evidence for a limited earth age of just thousands of years. The pervasive presence of carbon-14 in earth materials supports biblical creation.

Helium in zircons

Just as carbon-14 is found where it was not expected, similar results also occur for helium in granite. When granite rock forms underground from cooling magma, it locks in traces of radioac-

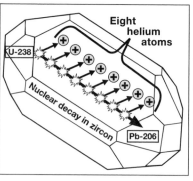

Figure 1: Zircon crystals occur inside granite. Uranium atoms within the zircons decay to helium and lead. Figures are taken from L. Vardiman, A. Snelling, and E. Chaffine, (Eds.), *Radioisotopes and the Age of the Earth*, Vol. 2, Institute for Creation Research and Creation Research Society, 2005.

tive elements, mainly uranium-238. This uranium decays through a series of steps and eventually becomes lead, Pb-206 (Figure 1). The half-life for U-238 is measured today at 4.47 billion years.

Along the path of uranium decay, eight alpha particles also are emitted. Many of these alpha particles capture an electron and become helium atoms. The uranium and resulting helium actually reside inside tiny crystals called zircons within the granite rock. These zircons are typically 50–75 microns, which is about the thickness of this page (Figure 2).

If a sample of granite is truly millions of years old, then most of the helium resulting from uranium decay should have escaped long ago from the rock. This follows because helium atoms are relatively small and mobile, and they do not combine with other elements. Recall how a helium balloon gradually loses its helium content and sinks to the floor.

Some years ago large amounts of helium were found still existing in "ancient" granite samples. The RATE team expanded this unexpected discovery. Granite rock samples were obtained from a mile un-

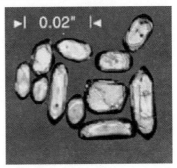

Figure 2: Dust-size zircon crystals extracted from granite rock are shown under polarized light. Photo by creation scientist Robert V. Gentry.

derground—the product of a government drilling project in New Mexico. This particular granite formation is dated at 1.5 billion years old. Zircon crystals were painstakingly separated from the rock after crushing. State-of-the-art instruments were then used to measure the helium content and also the ability of helium atoms to diffuse outward from the zircons. The results are shown in Figure 4. The vertical axis measures diffusion, the ease with which helium atoms exit the zircon crystals. The horizontal axis shows increasing temperature of the zircons as they were heated in the laboratory. The black circles show the actual RATE measurements of helium diffusion. This data trends upward because heat increases the movement of helium atoms. The upper squares are the calculated diffusion values, based on the amount of helium found in granite rocks, and an assumed timescale of 6,000 years. In contrast, the lower squares show the much smaller diffusion values required for the helium to be retained in the zircon crystals for a

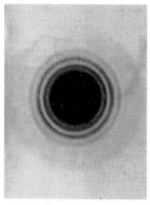

billion years. Clearly the creation model gives a much closer fit to the measured diffusion data. The long-age assumption is in conflict with the experimental diffusion data by a factor of at least 100,000.

These RATE studies indicate that helium atoms can only be retained in zircon crystals within granite for a few thousand years. Yet helium atoms are found in abundance inside granite zircons. The presence of this helium within granite points directly to a young earth.

Figure 3: A radiohalo burn due to radiation damage within a crystal. The inner black circle is 70 microns across, about the thickness of a sheet of paper.

Radiohalos

Radioactive decay, which occurs within crystalline rocks, may leave a permanent record in the form of radiohalos, or halos for short. These are tiny spherical regions of damage or "burns" in the crystal structure (Figure 3). The RATE team conducted a survey of halos in more than 100 granite rock samples collected from Finland, Australia and six western states. More than 40,000 halos

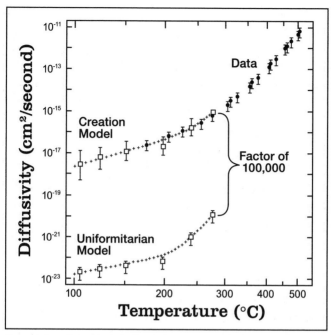

Figure 4: Data (large black dots) and theory (squares) showing the escape of helium atoms from zircon crystals.

were cataloged, and a fascinating trend became evident: most of the halos reside in granite rock which intrudes layers of Paleozoic and Mesozoic strata. RATE scientists believe that these sedimentary rock layers formed rapidly during the Genesis Flood. Upward-moving magma from tectonic activity intruded the layers and then cooled to become granite. The numerous radiohalos in this granite indicate that large-scale radioactivity accompanied the Flood event. This implies that radioactive decay was greatly accelerated during the year-long Flood.

The concept of accelerated nuclear decay was further explored by the RATE team. This is a radical idea because nuclear half-lives are assumed to be constant throughout history.

If nuclear lifetimes indeed varied in the past, then traditional radioisotope dating is fatally flawed. It is as if the world's clocks temporarily ran faster in the past, which makes their present readings unreliable. The mechanism of accelerated decay may have included temporary changes in the fundamental constants of nature. Further study is needed, including the Creator's possible reasons for modifying radioactivity.

Accelerated nuclear decay is one of several creation predictions that challenge the most basic assumptions of secular science. Similar predictions include evidence for *ex nihilo* creation, a young age for the earth, alteration of nature at the time of the Curse, the global Flood and the rapid formation of the earth's sedimentary rocks and fossil record. This reappraisal of earth history opens entirely new horizons for inquiry, research, and data interpretation.

Conclusion

RATE research further explored such topics as fission tracks, isochrons, nuclear theory and biblical data. Without exception the results give significant support for the young-earth model of earth history. The multi-year effort clearly has raised the bar on the quality and depth of creation research.

RATE members include: Steve Austin, John Baumgardner, Steve Boyd, Gene Chaffin, Don DeYoung, Russ Humphreys, Andrew Snelling, and Larry Vardiman.

Dr. Don DeYoung is chairman of Physical Science at Grace College, Winona Lake, Indiana. He is an active speaker for AiG and has written 14 books on Bible-science topics. Dr. DeYoung is currently president of the Creation Research Society with hundreds of members worldwide.

How Old Is the Earth?

by Bodie Hodge

*I*n the beginning God created the heavens and the earth (Genesis 1:1).

The question of the age of the earth has produced heated discussions on debate boards, in classrooms, on TV and radio, and in many churches, Christian colleges, and seminaries. The primary sides are:

- Young-earth proponents (biblical age of the earth and universe of about 6,000 years)[1]

- Old-earth proponents (secular age of the earth of about 4.5 billion years and a universe about 14 billion years old)[2]

The difference is immense! Let's give a little history of where these two basic calculations came from and which worldview is more reasonable.

Origin of the young-earth view

Simply put, it came from the Bible. Of course, the Bible doesn't say explicitly anywhere, "the earth is 6,000 years old." Good thing it doesn't; otherwise it would be out of date the following year. But we wouldn't expect an all-knowing God to make that kind of a mistake.

God gave us something better. In essence, He gave us a "birth certificate." For example, using my personal birth certificate, I can calculate how old I am at any point. It is similar with the earth. Genesis 1 says that the earth was created on the first day of creation (Genesis 1:1–5). From there, we can begin calculations of the age of the earth.

Let's do a rough calculation to show how this works. The age of the earth can be estimated by taking the first 5 days of creation (from earth's creation to Adam), then following the genealogies from Adam to Abraham in Genesis 5 and 11, then adding in the time from Abraham to today.

Adam was created on Day Six, so there were five days before him. If we add up the dates from Adam to Abraham, we get about 2,000 years, using the Masoretic Hebrew text of Genesis 5 and 11.[3] Whether Christian or secular, most scholars would agree that Abraham lived about 2000 BC (4,000 years ago).

So a simple calculation is:

$$
\begin{array}{r}
5 \text{ days} \\
+ \sim 2{,}000 \text{ years} \\
+ \sim 4{,}000 \text{ years} \\
\hline
\sim 6{,}000 \text{ years}
\end{array}
$$

At this point, the first five days are negligible. Quite a few people have done this calculation using the Masoretic text (which is what most English translations are based on) and, with careful attention to the biblical details, have arrived at the same time-frame of about 6,000 years, or about 4000 BC. Two of the most popular, and perhaps the best in my opinion, are a recent work by Dr. Floyd Jones and a much earlier book by Archbishop James Ussher (1581–1656):

Table 1. Jones and Ussher

	Who?	Age calculated	Reference and date
1	Archbishop James Ussher	4004 BC	The Annals of the World, 1658 A.D.[4]
2	Dr. Floyd Nolan Jones	4004 BC	The Chronology of the Old Testament, 1993 A.D.[5]

Often, there is a misconception that Ussher and Jones were

the only ones to do a chronology and arrive a date of about 6,000 years. However this is not the case at all. Jones gives a listing of several chronologists who have undertaken the task of calculating the age of the earth based on the Bible and their calculations range from 5501 to 3836 BC. A few are listed in Table 2.

Table 2. Chronologists' calculations according to Dr. Jones[6]

	Chronologist	When calculated?	Date BC
1	Julius Africanus	c. 240	5501
2	George Syncellus	c. 810	5492
3	John Jackson	1752	5426
4	Dr William Hales	c. 1830	5411
5	Eusebius	c. 330	5199
6	Marianus Scotus	c. 1070	4192
7	L. Condomanus	n/a	4141
8	Thomas Lydiat	c. 1600	4103
9	M. Michael Maestlinus	c. 1600	4079
10	J. Ricciolus	n/a	4062
11	Jacob Salianus	c. 1600	4053
12	H. Spondanus	c. 1600	4051
13	Martin Anstey	1913	4042
14	W. Lange	n/a	4041
15	E. Reinholt	n/a	4021
16	J. Cappellus	c. 1600	4005
17	E. Greswell	1830	4004
18	E. Faulstich	1986	4001
19	D. Petavius	c. 1627	3983
20	Frank Klassen	1975	3975
21	Becke	n/a	3974

22	Krentzeim	n/a	3971
23	W. Dolen	2003	3971
24	E. Reusnerus	n/a	3970
25	J. Claverius	n/a	3968
26	C. Longomontanus	c. 1600	3966
27	P. Melanchthon	c. 1550	3964
28	J. Haynlinus	n/a	3963
29	A. Salmeron	d. 1585	3958
30	J. Scaliger	d. 1609	3949
31	M. Beroaldus	c. 1575	3927
32	A. Helwigius	c. 1630	3836

As you will likely note from Table 2, the dates are not all 4004 BC. There are several reasons chronologists have different dates[7] but the two primary ones are:

1. Some used the Septuagint or another early translation, instead of the Hebrew Masoretic text. The Septuagint is a Greek translation of the Hebrew Old Testament, done about 250 BC by about 70 Jewish scholars (hence it is often cited as the LXX). It is good in most places, but appears to have a number of inaccuracies. For example, one relates to the Genesis chronologies where the LXX indicates that Methuselah would have lived past the Flood, without being on the Ark!

2. Several points in the biblical time-line are not straightforward to calculate. They require very careful study of more than one passage. These include exactly how much time the Israelites were in Egypt and what Terah's age was when Abraham was born. (See Jones's and Ussher's books for a detailed discussion of these difficulties.)

The first four in Table 2 (bolded) are calculated from the Septuagint, which gives ages for the patriarchs' firstborn much higher than the Masoretic text or the Samarian Pentateuch (another version from the Jews in Samaria just before Christ). Because of this, the LXX adds in extra time. Though the Samarian and Masoretic texts are much closer, they still have a couple of differences.

Table 3. Septuagint, Masoretic, and Samarian early patriarchal ages[8]

Name	Masoretic	Samarian Pentateuch	Septuagint
Adam	130	130	230
Seth	105	105	205
Enosh	90	90	190
Cainan	70	70	170
Mahalaleel	65	65	165
Jared	162	62	162
Enoch	65	65	165
Methuselah	187	67	167
Lamech	182	53	188
Noah	500	500	500

Using data from Table 2 (excluding the Septuagint calculations and including Jones and Ussher), the average date of the creation of the earth is 4045 BC. This still yields an average of about 6,000 years for the age of the earth.

Extra-biblical calculations for the age of the earth

Cultures throughout the world have kept track of history as

well. From a biblical perspective, we would expect the dates given for creation of the earth to align much closer to the biblical date than billions of years.

This is expected since everyone was descended from Noah and scattered from the Tower of Babel. Another expectation is that there should be some discrepancies among the age of the earth as people scattered throughout the world, taking their uninspired records or oral history to different parts of the globe.

Under the entry "creation," *Young's Analytical Concordance of the Bible*[9] lists William Hales's accumulation of dates of creation from many cultures and in most cases Hales says which authority gave the date.

Table 4: Selected dates by Hale for the age of the earth by various cultures

	Culture	Age, BC	Authority listed by Hales
1	Spain by Alfonso X	6984	Muller
2	Spain by Alfonso X	6484	Strauchius
3	India	6204	Gentil
4	India	6174	Arab Records
5	Babylon	6158	Bailly
6	Chinese	6157	Bailly
7	Greece by Diogenes Laertius	6138	Playfair
8	Egypt	6081	Bailly
9	Persia	5507	Bailly
10	Israel/Judea by Josephus	5555	Playfair
11	Israel/Judea by Josephus	5481	Jackson
12	Israel/Judea by Josephus	5402	Hales
13	Israel/Judea by Josephus	4698	University History
14	India	5369	Megasthenes
15	Babylon (Talmud)	5344	Petrus Alliacens

16	Vatican (Catholic using the Septuagint)	5270	N/A
17	Samaria	4427	Scaliger
18	German, Holy Roman Empire by Johannes Kepler[10]	3993	Playfair
19	German, reformer by Martin Luther	3961	N/A
20	Israel/Judea by computation	3760	Strauchius
21	Israel/Judea by Rabbi Lipman	3616	University History

These were not the only ones. Historian Bill Cooper's research in *After the Flood* provides intriguing dates from several ancient cultures.[11] The first is that of the Anglo-Saxons, whose history has 5,200 years from creation to Christ, according to the Laud and Parker Chronicles. Cooper's research also indicated that Nennius' record of the ancient British history has 5,228 years from creation to Christ. The Irish chronology has a date of about 4000 BC for creation which is surprisingly close to Ussher and Jones! Even the Mayans had a date for the Flood of 3113 BC.

This meticulous work of many historians should not be ignored. Their dates of only thousands of years are good support for the biblical date of about 6,000 years, but not for billions of years.

Origin of the old-earth view

Prior to the 1700s, few believed in an old earth. The approximate 6,000-year age for the earth was challenged only rather recently, beginning in the late 18th century. These opponents of the biblical chronology essentially left God out of the picture. Three of the old-earth advocates included Comte de Buffon, who thought the earth was at least 75,000 years old. Pièrre LaPlace imagined an indefinite but very long history. And Jean Lamarck also proposed long ages.[12]

However, the idea of millions of years really took hold in geology when men like Abraham Werner, James Hutton, William Smith, Georges Cuvier, and Charles Lyell used their interpretations of geology as the standard, rather than the Bible. Werner estimated the age of the earth at about one million years. Smith and Cuvier believed untold ages were needed for the formation of rock layers. Hutton said he could see no geological evidence of a beginning of the earth; and building on Hutton's thinking, Lyell advocated "millions of years."[13]

From these men and others came the consensus view that the geologic layers were laid down slowly over long periods of time based on the rates we see them accumulating today. Hutton said:

The past history of our globe must be explained by what can be seen to be happening now. ... No powers are to be employed that are not natural to the globe, no action to be admitted except those of which we know the principle.[14]

This viewpoint is called naturalistic uniformitarianism, and would exclude any major catastrophes like Noah's Flood. Though some, such as Cuvier and Smith, believed in multiple catastrophes separated by long periods of time, the uniformitarian concept became the ruling dogma in geology.

Thinking biblically, we can see that the global Flood in Genesis 6–8 would wipe away the concept of millions of years, for this Flood would explain massive amounts of fossil layers.

Most Christians fail to realize that if there was a global Flood, it would rip up many of the previous rock layers and redeposit them elsewhere, destroying the previous fragile contents. This would destroy any evidence of alleged millions of years anyway. So the rock layers can theoretically represent the evidence of either millions of years or a global Flood, but not both. Sadly, by about 1840 even most of the Church had accepted the dogmatic claims of the secular geologists and rejected the global Flood and the biblical age of the earth.

After Lyell, in 1899, Lord Kelvin (William Thomson) calculated the age of the earth, based on the cooling rate of a molten sphere, at a maximum of about 20–40 million years (this was revised from his earlier calculation of 100 million years in 1862).[15] With the development of radiometric dating in the early 20th century, the age of the earth expanded radically. In 1913 Arthur Holmes' book, *The Age of the Earth,* gave an age of 1.6 billion years.[16] Since then, the supposed age of the earth has expanded to its present estimate of about 4.5 billion years (and about 14 billion years for the universe).

Table 5. Summary of the old-earth proponents for long ages

Who?	Age of the earth	When was this?
Comte de Buffon	78 thousand years old	1779
Abraham Werner	1 million years	1786
James Hutton	Perhaps eternal, long Ages	1795
Pièrre LaPlace	Long ages	1796
Jean Lamarck	Long ages	1809
William Smith	Long ages	1835
Georges Cuvier	Long ages	1812
Charles Lyell	Millions of years	1830–1833
Lord Kelvin	20-100 million years	1862–1899
Arthur Holmes	1.6 billion years	1913

But there is growing scientific evidence that radiometric dating methods are completely unreliable.[17]

Christians who have felt compelled to accept the millions of years as fact and try to fit them in the Bible need to become aware of this evidence. It confirms that the Bible's history is giving us the true age of the creation.

Today, secular geologists will allow some catastrophic events into their thinking as an explanation for what they see in the rocks. But uniformitarian thinking is still widespread and secular geologists will seemingly never entertain the idea of the global catastrophic Flood of Noah's day.

The age of the earth debate ultimately comes down to this foundational question. Are we trusting man's imperfect and changing ideas and assumptions about the past or trusting God's perfectly accurate eyewitness account of the past, including the creation of the world, Noah's global Flood and the age of the earth?

Uniformitarian methods for dating the age of the earth

Radiometric dating was the culminating factor that led to the belief in billions of years for earth history. However, radiometric dating methods are not the only uniformitarian methods. Any radiometric dating model or other uniformitarian dating method can and does have problems as referenced before (Reference 16). All uniformitarian dating methods make assumptions. The assumptions related to radiometric dating can be seen in these questions:

1. Initial amounts?

2. Was any parent amount added?

3. Was any daughter amount added?

4. Was any parent amount removed?

5. Was any daughter amount removed?

6. Has the rate changed?

If the assumptions are truly accurate, then uniformitarian dates should agree with radiometric dating across the board for the same event. However, radiometric dates often disagree with dates obtained from other uniformitarian dating methods for the age of the earth, such as the influx of salts into the ocean, the rate of decay of the earth's magnetic field, the growth rate of human population, etc.[18]

Henry Morris accumulated a list of 68 uniformitarian estimates for the age of the earth by Christian and secular sources.[19] The current accepted age of the earth is about 4.54 billion years based on radiometric dating meteorites,[20] so keep this in mind when viewing Table 6.

Table 6. Uniformitarian estimates for earth's age accumulated by Dr Henry Morris

	Number of uniformitarian methods[21]
0–10,000 years	23
>10,000–100,000 years	10
>100,000–1 million years	11
>1 million–500 million years	23
>500 million–4 billion years	0
>4 billion–5 billion years	0

As you can see, uniformitarian maximum ages for the earth obtained from other methods are nowhere near the 4.5 billion years estimated by radiometric dating; of the other methods only two calculated dates were as much as 500 million years.

Some radiometric dating methods completely undermine other radiometric dates too. One such example is carbon-14 (^{14}C) dating. As long as an organism is alive it takes in ^{14}C and ^{12}C from the atmosphere; however when it dies, it will stop. Since ^{14}C is radioactive (decays into ^{14}N), the amount of ^{14}C in a dead organism gets less and less over time. Carbon-14 dates are determined from the measured ratio of radioactive carbon-14 to normal carbon-12 (^{14}C/^{12}C). Used on samples which were once alive, such as wood or bone, the measured ^{14}C/^{12}C ratio is compared with the ratio in living things today.

Now, ^{14}C has a derived half-life of less than 6,000 years, so it should all have decayed into nitrogen by 100,000 years, at the maximum.[22] Some things, such as wood trapped in lava flows, that are said to be millions of years old by other radiometric dating methods still have ^{14}C in them.[23] If the items were really millions of years old, then they shouldn't have any traces of ^{14}C. Coal and diamonds, which are found in or sandwiched between rock layers allegedly millions of years old, have been shown to have ^{14}C ages of only tens of thousands of years.[24] So which date, if any, is correct? The diamonds or coal can't be millions of years old if they have any traces of ^{14}C still in them. So this shows that these dating methods are completely unreliable and indicates that the presumed assumptions in the methods are erroneous.

Similar kinds of problems are seen in the case of potassium-argon dating, which is considered one of the most reliable methods. Dr. Andrew Snelling, a geologist, points out several of these problems with potassium-argon, as seen in Table 7.[24]

Table 7. Potassium-argon dates in error

Volcanic eruption	When the rock formed	Date by radiometric dating
Mt Etna basalt, Sicily	122 BC	170,000–330,000 years old
Mt Etna basalt, Sicily	AD 1972	210,000–490,000 years old
Mt St. Helens, Washington	AD 1986	300,000–400,000 years old
Hualalai basalt, Hawaii	AD 1800–1801	1.44–1.76 million years old
Mt Ngauruhoe, New Zealand	AD 1954	3.3–3.7 million years old
Kilauea Iki basalt, Hawaii	AD 1959	1.7–15.3 million years old

These and other examples raise a critical question. If radiometric dating fails to get an accurate date on something of which we *do* know the true age, then how can it be trusted to give us the correct age for rocks that had no human observers to record when they formed? If the methods don't work on rocks of known age, it is most unreasonable to trust that they work on rocks of unknown age. It is far more rational to trust the Word of the God who created the world, knows its history perfectly, and has revealed sufficient information in the Bible for us to understand that history and the age of the creation.

Conclusion

When we start our thinking with God's Word, we see that the world is about 6,000 years old. When we rely on man's fallible (and often demonstrably false) dating methods, we can get a confusing range of ages from a few thousand to billions of years, though the vast majority of methods do not give dates even close to billions.

Cultures around the world give an age of the earth which confirms what the Bible teaches. Radiometric dates, on the other hand, have been shown to be wildly in error.

The age of the earth ultimately comes down to a matter of trust—it's a worldview issue. Will you trust what an all-knowing God says on the subject or will you trust imperfect man's assumptions and imaginations about the past that regularly are changing?

> Thus says the LORD: "Heaven is My throne, and earth is My footstool. Where is the house that you will build Me? And where is the place of My rest? For all those things My hand has made, and all those things exist," says the LORD. "But on this one will I look: On him who is poor and of a contrite spirit, and who trembles at My word" (Isaiah 66:1–2).

1. Not all young-earth creationists agree on this age. Some believe that there may be small gaps in the genealogies of Genesis 5 and 11, and put the maximum age of the earth at about 10,000—12,000 years.

2. Some of these old-earth proponents accept molecules-to-man biological evolution and so are called theistic evolutionists. Others reject neo-Darwinian evolution, but accept the evolutionary time-scale for stellar and geological evolution, and hence agree with the evolutionary order of events in history.

3. Russell Grigg, "Meeting the Ancestors," *Creation* 25:2 (March 2003):13–15.

4. James Ussher, *The Annals of the World* (Green Forest, Arkansas: Master Books, 2003), translated by Larry and Marion Pierce.

5. Floyd Nolan Jones, *Chronology of the Old Testament* (Green Forest, Arkansas: Master Books, 2005).

6. Ibid., 26.

7. Others would include gaps in the chronology based on the presences of an extra Cainan in Luke 3:36. But there are good reasons this should be left out. It is included in late copies of the Septuagint. But early copies of the LXX do not have it, so it was added later. The English 18th-century Hebrew expert John Gill points out: "This Cainan is not mentioned by Moses in Gen 11:12 nor has he ever appeared in any Hebrew copy of the Old Testament, nor in the Samaritan version, nor in the Targum; nor is he mentioned by Josephus, nor in 1Chron 1:24 where the genealogy is repeated; nor is it in Beza's most ancient Greek copy of Luke: it indeed stands in the present copies of the Septuagint, but was not originally there; and therefore could not be taken by Luke from thence, but seems to be owing to some early negligent transcriber of Luke's Gospel, and since put into the Septuagint to give it authority: I say "early," because it is in many Greek copies, and in the Vulgate Latin, and all the Oriental versions, even in the Syriac, the oldest of them; but ought not to stand neither in the text, nor in any version: for certain it is, there never was such a Cainan, the son of Arphaxad, for Salah was his son; and with him the next words should be connected," bible.crosswalk.com/Commentaries/GillsExpositionoftheBible/gil.cgi?book=lu&chapter=003&verse=036&next=037&prev=035

8. Biblical chronogenealogies, *TJ* 17 no. 3 (2003):14–18.

9. Robert Young, *Young's Analytical Concordance to the Bible* (Peadoby, Massachussets: Hendrickson, 1996), referring to William Hales, *A New Analysis of Chronology and Geography, History and Prophecy* (1830), vol. 1, 210.

10. Luther, Kepler, Lipman, and the Jewish computation likely used biblical texts to determine the date.

11. Bill Cooper, *After the Flood* (UK: New Wine Press, 1995), 122–129.

12. Terry Mortenson, "The origin of old-earth geology and its ramifications for life in the 21st century," *TJ* 18 no. 1 (2004):22–26, online at www.answersingenesis.org/tj/v18/i1/oldearth.asp

13. James Hutton, *Theory of the earth*, Trans. of Roy. Soc. of Edinburgh, 1785; quoted in A. Holmes, *Principles of Physical Geology* (UK: Thomas Nelson & Sons Ltd., 1965), 43–44.

14. "William Thompson: king of Victorian physics," Mark McCartney, Physics Web, December 2002, online at physicsweb.org/articles/world/15/12/6.

15. Terry Mortenson, "The history of the development of the geological column," in Michael Oard and John Reed, eds., *The Geologic Column* (CRS, 2006).

16. For articles at the layman's level see "Radiometric Dating Questions and Answers," online at www.answersingenesis.org/home/area/faq/dating.asp. For a technical discussion see Larry Vardiman, Eugene Chaffin, and Andrew Snelling, eds., *Radioisotopes and the Age of the Earth Volume 2*, (El Cajon, Califonia: Institute for Creation Research/Creation Research Society, 2005). See also "Half-Life Heresy," *New Scientist* (21 Oct. 2006), 36–39, Abstract

online at www.newscientist.com/channel/fundamentals/mg19225741.100-halflife-heresy-accelerating-radioactive-decay.html.

17. Russell Humphrey, "Evidence for a Young World," *Impact* #384, Institute for Creation Research, June 2005, online at www.answersingenesis.org/docs/4005.asp

18. Henry M. Morris, *The New Defender's Study Bible* (Nashville, Tennessee: World Publishing, 2006), pp. 2076–2079.

19. "The Age of the Earth," USGS, geology.wr.usgs.gov/parks/gtime/ageofearth.html.

20. When a range of ages is given, the maximum age was used, to be generous to the evolutionists. In one case, the date was uncertain so it was not used in this tally, so the total estimates used were 67. A few on the list had reference to Saturn, the Sun, etc., but since biblically-speaking the earth is older than these, dates related to them were used.

21. This does not mean that a ^{14}C date of 50,000 or 100,000 would be entirely trustworthy. I am only using this to highlight the mistaken assumptions behind uniformitarian dating methods.

22. Andrew Snelling, "Conflicting 'ages' of Tertiary basalt and contained fossilized wood, Crinum, Central Queensland Australia," *Technical Journal* 14 no. 2 (2000):99-122.

23. J. Baumgardner, "^{14}C Evidence for a Recent Global Flood and a Young Earth," in Vardiman et al., *Radioisotopes and the Age of the Earth: Results of a Young-Earth Creationist Research Initiative* (Santee, California: Institute for Creation Research, and Chino Valley, Arizona: Creation Research Society, 2005), pp.587–630.

24. Andrew Snelling, "Excess Argon: The 'Achilles' Heel' of Potassium-Argon and Argon-Argon Dating of Volcanic Rocks," *Impact* #307, Institute for Creation Research, online at www.icr.org/index.php?module=articles&action=view&ID=436.

Bodie Hodge attended Southern Illinois University at Carbondale (SIUC) and received a BS and MS (in 1996 and 1998 respectively) there in mechanical engineering. His specialty was a subset of mechanical engineering based in advanced materials processing, particularly starting powders.

Bodie conducted research for his master's degree through a grant from Lockheed Martin and developed a New Method of Production of Submicron Titanium Diboride. The new process was able to make titanium diboride cheaper, faster and with higher quality. This technology is essential for some nanotechnologies.

Currently, Bodie is a speaker, writer, and researcher in AiG's Outreach Department.

The Heavens Declare a Young Solar System

by Ron Samec

Psalm 19 tells us that the heavens declare the glory of God. But what do the heavens declare about the age of the universe? Recent observations confirm that the universe is only a few thousand years old, as the Bible says.

The existence of comets

Comets are small, low density, icy "asteroids" that orbit the sun. But their lifetime is limited. As they come near the sun, some of their icy material is vaporized and blown away—forming a "tail."

The actual body of the comet, called the "nucleus," is very small, ranging from 1 to 30 miles (1–50 km) in diameter. It also

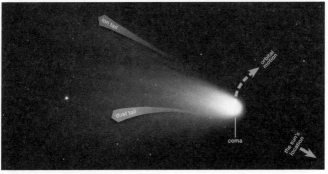

Anatomy of a Comet: A comet is a ball of ice and rocky dust particles (as seen in this image of Hale-Bopp). The ion tail (blue) points away from the sun and is blown back by its interaction with solar wind. The dust tail (yellow-white) is swept back by radiation pressure. It sweeps behind the comet due to its orbital motion around the sun.

Death of a Comet: These time-lapse images show the disintegration of the Schwassmann–Wachmann 3 (S-W 3) comet. This comet disintegrated over the past several decades. The Hubble telescope captured detailed photos of its breakup.

has very low density, certainly less than that of water. Earth-based observers cannot see the nucleus. Instead they see only the gases and dust particles that come from the nucleus, including a large glowing gas ball, called a coma, and the ion and dust tails. The gas (ion) tail is blown away from the sun by solar wind, and the dust tail is forced back by the pressure of photons. The presence of tails and comas tells us that comets are constantly losing mass.

Comets, as well as their orbits, are greatly affected by the planets. For instance, Jupiter has corralled about 45 comets within its orbit and evidently can destroy comets; Jupiter's gravitational field can cause comets to break apart and even collide with the planet itself. In addition, the SOHO spacecraft has regularly recorded comets being completely destroyed as they encounter the sun.

Many comets have been observed to break up or at least partially disintegrate. In 1852 Comet Biela was observed to divide in two, and in 1872, a meteor shower appeared in its place. Indeed, nearly all meteor showers are linked to the disintegration of known comets.

It is apparent that comets are temporary. And from their orbits, we find that comets do not just fall in from interplanetary space. They appear to be true members of the solar system, and so they are limited in number. If the solar system were 4.6 billion years old, our complete supply of comets should have been exhausted long ago. Instead, comets are plentiful.

To resolve this challenge, uniformitarian astronomers believe that long-period comets arise from the Oort cloud, a hypothesized cloud of comet nuclei with a radius of about 50,000 AU (an astronomical unit is the average distance between the earth and sun). Evolutionists Carl Sagan and Ann Druvan admit in their book entitled *Comet*, "Many scientific papers are written each year about the Oort Cloud, its properties, its origin, its evolution. Yet there is not yet a shred of direct observational evidence for its existence."

Likewise, the shorter period comets are believed to come from the Kuiper belt, a disk of icy asteroids beginning at the orbit of Pluto (40 AU) and extending out to about 55 AU. But such objects have different characteristics from the comets, so they cannot explain the wealth of comets we see today.

The moon is still alive

The moon is very much alive, geologically speaking. Ever since telescopes have been available, observers have been reporting many color changes, bright and colored spots and streaks, clouds, hazes, veils, and other phenomena on the moon. Since these phenomena

Aristarchus Region of the Moon: Over 300 transient lunar phenomena have occurred in the Aristarchus region of the moon, indicating that the moon is young, just as the Bible says.

are short lived, they are called Transient Lunar Phenomena (TLP). These speak of geologic activity.

From 1900 to 1960, many of these observations were dismissed and ignored because the prevailing belief was that the moon is 4.5 billion years old and has been geologically dead for the last 3 billion years. (As the argument went, since the moon is about one-fourth of the size of the earth, heavy masses would fall to the center, the moon would cool much faster than the earth, and no magma would be left.) But the number of TLP observations became so overwhelming that mainline publications began to discuss them. In 1968, NASA published the *Chronological Catalog of Reported Lunar Events.*

As early as March 1787, William Herschel, the discoverer of Uranus and an ardent lunar observer, reported, "I perceive three volcanoes in different places of the dark side of the moon. Two of them are either extinct, or otherwise in a state of going to break out. . . . The third shows an actual eruption of fire, or luminous matter." The next night he continued, "The volcano burns with greater violence than last night. I believe the diameter . . . to be about three miles." More than 300 TLP's have been seen in the Aristarchus region alone. This and hundreds of similar observations point to the youthfulness of the moon, as the Bible tells us.

Jupiter and Neptune are still so hot

We have been taught that solar system bodies shine only by reflected light. Is this true? No, not for the Jovian gas giants, Jupiter and Neptune. In fact, the power excess for Jupiter is 3×10^{17} watts.[1] Jupiter actually radiates nearly twice as much power as it receives from the sun, but mostly in the infrared. That's enough power to continuously burn three million-billion 100-watt light bulbs. Saturn puts out half the energy but is one-quarter the mass, so it produces twice the energy per unit mass as Jupiter does. Neptune gives off well over twice as much energy as it receives. Uranus's energy production is somewhat in doubt, but even it appears to give off slightly more than it receives. This means that each of these three planets has an alternate energy source. What is it?

Jupiter puts out nearly twice the energy it receives from the sun. This makes sense if the planet is only thousands of years old.

The usual explanation for Jupiter's extra energy is that it is shrinking. This converts gravitational energy into internal heat and radiation. Can this explain the extra energy? No. Shrinkage alone does not produce enough energy. Others have said that helium is raining down on the core, releasing additional gravitational energy. While that may be the explanation for Saturn and Uranus, whose surfaces are helium depleted, observations of the vibrations of the surface (asteroseismology) have shown this is not correct for Jupiter.[2]

Researchers[3] have hypothesized that nuclear reactions are occurring in the core of Jupiter as a result of burning deuterium (heavy hydrogen). This requires a core temperature of 160,000 K, some 8 times hotter than the present models of Jupiter. Will this produce the extra energy? To make this work, most of the deuterium available throughout Jupiter had to simultaneously descend to its core when Jupiter formed so the deuterium would be hot enough to ignite. Once it ignited, it would burn happily for 10 billion years or more and keep Jupiter hot. This would give us a hot Jupiter like the one we see today. At first, this solution appears to be ingenious. The snag is that the deuterium layer has to assemble itself at just the right time and at the right place to sustain Jupiter's core temperature. The same unlikely event must be repeated on Neptune.

The definition of a star is any large, self-gravitating gaseous sphere with continued nuclear reactions in its core. Our sun is a star. It burns hydrogen in its core. But if Jupiter and Neptune have nuclear reactions in their cores, then they are dwarf suns. There would be three suns in our solar system.

There is a simpler explanation. God created the Jovian planets. The heat energy comes from the creative work of God and any gravitational energy produced since then. Since they are young and quite massive, the Jovian planets have not had time to cool down. Are hot Jovian planets a problem to creationists? Absolutely not! They are only a problem to evolutionists.

Fast facts

- Spiral galaxies rotate much too quickly for an old universe. They would be twisted beyond recognition if they were really as old as secular astronomers claim.
- The magnetic fields of planets and moons in our solar system are consistent with their age of a few thousand years, but are much too strong for an age of billions of years.
- The debris shed by disintegrating comets is what causes meteor showers. Since earth intersects such a debris field once each year, most meteor showers are annual.

A final word

The Bible can be trusted in every area it addresses, including its scientific and historical truth. It is God's Book, which means what it says in a plain, forthright manner. While the Bible's revealed insights about science and history glorify the Creator and help us know Him better, its main purpose is to convey to people, like you and me, our need of Jesus Christ as Savior and God's desire for us to live a fulfilled, joyful life with Him.